God

Steps In

God
Steps In

PASTOR LERONE DINNALL

GOD STEPS IN

iUniverse books may be ordered through booksellers or by contacting:

iUniverse
1663 Liberty Drive
Bloomington, IN 47403
www.iuniverse.com
1-800-Authors (1-800-288-4677)

ISBN: 978-1-5320-4932-3 (sc)
ISBN: 978-1-5320-4933-0 (e)

Print information available on the last page.

iUniverse rev. date: 10/22/2018

A TRIBUTE

"To MY SPIRITUAL AND Physical Father, the Late Bishop Austin Whitfield and also to his wife Lady Whitfield that is still alive. Of which without their Guidance in the Ministry and the Word of God along with their support, My life to become a Pastor would not be possible".

INTRODUCTION

ALL GLORY, HONOR AND Praise goes to Our Father; The God of Abraham, The God of Isaac, The God of Israel; Jesus Christ The Lamb of God, by whom all things Exist, and through Him was this Book made possible for His Messages and Revelations to reach the Minds and Hearts of those who are Destined to become The Children of The Kingdom of God.

God Steps In is a Spiritual Map for all People, Nations, Cultures and Languages, to show forth the pathway that each man would have to walk, in order to align himself and his Generation in the Requirements of God, that will allow present and future Generations to know what it takes to remain in Favor with The God of The Universe.

This Book is geared towards opening the Minds of People, to allow us to first Understand that there is only one pathway that People, Nations and Languages can embrace, to allow The God of The Universe to Release Forgiveness; and once we are forgiven by God, Then and only then, will we be able to receive as a People the experience of True Peace that springs from The Father of Love.

The Generation that is currently living now, need to be Born in

The Understanding very quickly, to know that unless we Return to God, then it is certain, there will not be a future for our Generations to Inherit. Therefore the Beginning of this Book seeks to bring God's People back to Foundation; to allow for us to Understand that every Journey that leads back to The Will of God must involve Repentance.

Climbing the Ladder of this Book we will discover that after Repentance, the Free Will of God's People has to be Maintained in The Discipline of God's Will, to ensure that we are on track to Inherit The Kingdom of God. Therefore it will be observed that the Message of this Book moves on, to allow us to understand more about God's Covenant, Commandment and Vows.

It is identified that Family plays a Major role in the Moral of Society, thus it is Manifested within this Book four Messages that speaks towards The Development of Families; The Maintenance of the Family Circle, and also the Preserving of the Family Structure for Future Generations. This section of The Book is also Garnished with Special Prayers for God's People and their Generations to follow.

God Steps in seek to allow Christians and also people that are not yet saved, to know for a Fact that if we are Destined in God's Will to be a part of God's Kingdom, no matter what we are going through, we will Identify somewhere on The pathway of this Journey The Manifestation of The Heavily Father, Stepping into our Condition, to Reveal The Power of His Might for all those who believe on His Name. Therefore within this Book it is identified who a Child of God Truly is, and also Who it is that Represents each Child of God.

It is identified that Training must now be the watch word for a Child of God, and that Training has to be Maintained throughout the Generation of that Child of God, to ensure that once we have received of God's Divine Favored Blessing; we will become Knowledgeable to know exactly what we need to do, to ensure that we are able to keep that which God Has Released as Blessing for our Generation. Therefore this Book seeks to allow us to understand The Seven Discipline, The Secret of how to remain Blessed.

Before reaching the Climax of this Book, it is Revealed through Messages by God to explain exactly what is the TEST that each

Child of God must face. After reading through the experience of the Test, we are greeted with a journey to know how important it is to Trust in God. For the Conclusion of the Messages from this Book, The Children of God are served with A Divine Reminder, to let us understand how Important we are in The Eyes of The Heavily Father, just as long as we continue on the pathway to follow The Disciplines of God Almighty. This Final Message is known as God's Favor.

Receive of God's Anointing, through the Messages that He has Revealed in This Book for yourself, and for your Generation, God Bless.

CONTENTS

REPENTANCE

Message # 83

Date Started September 14, 2017
Date Finalized September 15, 2017.

I GREET THE ALMIGHTY Father, Creator of the Universe; in The Name of Jesus Christ let God be known throughout all Nations, Languages and Tongues, that He is God. I'm excited to be speaking on this Topic, reason being, I know that this Topic will help a lot of people, including those of us who are Saints. Ignorance is the main Enemy for Christians, because we don't know, we continue to walk and live our lives in circles; not achieving nor climbing the Ladder of Spirituality, to become what God would have for us to Truly become.

Let us seek to find out the Foundation of what this Topic seeks to establish. According to the Webster's Dictionary, the word Repentance is coming from the word Repent, which is a Verb, which means that this state of Mind and conduct requires Action from the Individual that is in the process of Repentance. The Dictionary's Meaning States: "TO FEEL REGRETFUL OR CONTRITE FOR PAST CONDUCTS: TO REPENT OF AN ACT. TO BE PENITENT FOR ONE'S SINS AND SEEK TO CHANGE ONE'S LIFE FOR THE BETTER". The

Student Bible Dictionary states Repentance as: "A GODLY GRIEF THAT CHANGES MIND, HEART, AND LIFE THROUGH TRUST IN CHRIST".

Now it is important to understand that, that which causes the need for Repentance is an act of Sin and Continual Sin. Now when it is found that there is no more carpet to sweep the sin under that it will not be Revealed; those Sin now becomes a scent of Bad Odor in The Nostril of God, of which He will no more Accept the continuation of such activities of Sin; therefore when the Limit has been past, it now spells the word Action from God, of which God cannot take Action to execute Judgment unless He first follow the Constitution of His own Words, to ensure that there is first a Warning. A Warning that is sent through different Messengers; a Warning that is Revealed in Different Times; a Warning that is Revealed in different Seasons. And it must be noted that God is Justified in every Action that God has Caused to take place in the lives of People, Nations, Languages and also Saints.

The Lord has Revealed that there is a period of time that is set, that those who are to be warned, would have had enough time to make sure that they can get their house in order; to the effect that they can actually prevent what is to happen in their lives, by the only means of Repentance. Now when it is that God have Seen that such an individual choose to now change from their lifestyle of Sin, to now pattern a lifestyle that God would Accept; then and only then will God also Repent of what He was Destined to fulfill in that Individual's life. Because the only reason for the Warning to Repent is because there is a Sin or Sins that continues to take effect in that person's life. The Lord has Revealed that once the seed of warning has been sent, whether that person choose to accept the warning or not, in God's Eye, that warning has been Delivered. Now The Lord Revealed that from the time that the First warning has been sent, to the actual time that The Lord will now Act; will span a period of Three (3) to Five (5) years; of which because The Lord is Merciful in Judgment, the hearts of those who are called to Repentance, if they refuse to Repent, then they would have accepted their own conclusion to think that if The Lord was truly going to do what He Said He is going to do, then it should have happen a long time; thus causing that person to remain in the condition to continue to Sin. The Book of Ecclesiastes Chapter 8:11 States: "BECAUSE SENTENCE AGAINST AN EVIL WORK IS NOT EXECUTED SPEEDILY, THEREFORE THE HEART OF THE SONS OF MEN IS FULLY SET IN THEM TO DO EVIL".

There is a False Cloak of covering that Christians have long time been embracing; and that False Hope it is to be of the Mind frame that once we have been Baptized and going to Church, we have no more Sins; even if it is found that we have made a mistake that causes us to Sin; such an event will not be mentioned by us, because we have Doctrinated ourselves to believe that if we admit that we have Sinned, it would have taken away the Value of our Christian walk. I would be the first person to admit that I have Sinned, because after I have Repented and confess to God, and have received of my forgiveness, what can the other Saints, Pastors, Missionaries, Ministers, Bishops, and even those in the World, what can they now do to me? The last time I check, I believed that Salvation was to Save us from Damnation; therefore my Aim is not to remain on this Earth or in the Church Assembly, but to make sure that I can reach Heaven. And if it takes me Four Hundred and ninety times in a day to ask God to forgive me and then to change, then I'm willing to do just that, because my seat is already in Heaven. Christians must come to the Understanding that Earth, the Church, our Surroundings is our Process to get to Heaven; and if we don't go through the Process, then we have Failed the Test of our Training Ground to prepare and to carry us into Heaven. We can't cut short the Process, neither can we give back a Test that has our Name on the paper for our lives.

We need to understand that it takes time to become Perfect in this Christian walk, and not every direction of our pathway is going to become perfect at the same time. There is going to be some challenges that is going to require years of Repentance, because we just have not yet mastered what we should be doing. The whole life span of a Christian walk, will require a lifetime for the Prayer of

Confession of Sins, until we have reached the Perfect man. There are some Christians that have Perfected not to tell lies, but at the same time that same Christian is struggling with the spirit that cause them to Lust. Another Christian will never commit Adultery, because they just can't see themselves hurting God and their Partner, and also they respect themselves, but at the same time, that same Christian is struggling with the Red Eye Monster. Therefore seeing all these evidence; can we conclude that Repentance is and must be a Daily Ritual! I ask The Lord to forgive me for the Sins that I know not about; because I want to make certain that I have not past over one Sin, because one Sin can be compared to one spot on my Garment, of which if there is but just one spot, then I'm in Big Trouble.

There is found in the Church at present, a whole lot of believers that have not yet Repented, and that's the reason why it is at present that there is a whole lot of problems in The Church; that's the main reason why there is no longer The Glory of God in The House of God; that's the reason why there is no longer any Miracles, No Healing, No Victory for God's People, because all God Sees is Sin and Sin and more Sin coming before Him to offer the Sacrifice which will never be Accepted by God. If we should do a survey on Christians, by asking randomly; and the Question would be: "WHAT DO YOU LOVE ABOUT CHURCH OR CHRISTIANITY". We would observe that there would only be 10% which represent the Tithes of Saints for God that would give a response that says:

"I LOVE THAT I'VE NOW BECOME HOLY".

Many will say: "I LOVE THE PASTOR, I LOVE THE MEMBERS, I LOVE THE MUSIC, I LOVE THE CHOIR, I LOVE THE BENEFITS".

All these things are good to love, but the main emphasis must be God; if the Focus for Christianity is not God, then we are on Sinking Sand. For those of us that are Leaders for God, it is important to understand that a Church cannot Stand with members that have not yet Repented. It would be compared to using sticks which would represent unrighteousness to be the Pillars of a Righteous House. Un-repented, Unrighteous members are to be compared to Tools that are broken, thus they cannot fulfill their purpose, that's a Fact! We must try to remember the story of Cain and Abel; Cain offered his Offering and it was Rejected by God. Abel offered his Offering and it was Accepted by God. So is it in The Church. An Un-Repented, Unrighteous Soul will prevent The Glory of God to be Released. Each day that is faced, God has a Glory that is fixed to be Released, that His People can enjoy the benefits of the land; therefore it is of great necessity that God's People always seek to find themselves in a Position that we are Ready Waiting for The Glory to be Released. Sanctify before the Sacrifice must now be the Watch Word of God's People; because if we cannot find ourselves to be Clean which includes Repentance, how are we going to be able to find ourselves in the Position to offer the Sacrifice that God will Accept? Think about that!

St John Chapter 9:31 Says: "NOW WE KNOW THAT GOD HEARETH NOT SINNERS: BUT IF ANY MAN BE A WORSHIPPER OF GOD, AND DOETH HIS WILL, HIM HE HEARETH". What is my view on this Scripture? According to The Revelations that I have Received from God, this is what God Explained: The Scripture is 100% True; The Lord Explained that there are many in the World presently that are judged to be a Sinner according to man's eye and man's judgment; The Lord Explained that for those who are judged as a sinner because they don't follow certain guidelines instructed by man; The Lord Explained that they are His Believers; and being His Believers, His Eyes are constantly upon them, to answer their request to prove Himself a Faithful God. The Lord Reveals that there are Believers at different levels; meaning that there will be some believers that are known because they are seen going to Church, but the big question is this, what about those believers who has a secret Relationship with God, based on the Fact that they have found themselves to be in some Delicate Positions in life. Nicodemus was one of those Secret Believers, he couldn't openly admit that he was a follower, but in his heart he knew what he believed in. On the other hand is the Sinners; now it is important for us to Understand who a Sinner is, and what a Sinner continue to do, that displeases the very

Presence of The Almighty God, that it is found, that the very breath of such a Sinner will Chase away The Presence of God.

Genesis Chapter 6:5-6 Says: "AND GOD SAW THAT THE WICKEDNESS OF MAN WAS GREAT IN THE EARTH, AND THAT EVERY IMAGINATION OF THE THOUGHTS OF HIS HEART WAS ONLY EVIL CONTINUALLY. AND IT REPENTED THE LORD THAT HE HAD MADE MAN ON THE EARTH; AND IT GRIEVED HIM AT HIS HEART".

Psalms 66:18 Says: "IF I REGARD INIQUITY IN MY HEART, THE LORD WILL NOT HEAR ME".

Job 27:8-10 Says: "FOR WHAT IS THE HOPE OF THE HYPOCRITE, THOUGH HE HATH GAINED, WHEN GOD TAKETH AWAY HIS SOUL? WILL GOD HEAR HIS CRY WHEN TROUBLE COMETH UPON HIM? WILL HE DELIGHT HIMSELF IN THE ALMIGHTY? WILL HE ALWAYS CALL UPON GOD?"

Psalms 34:12-16 Says: "WHAT MAN IS HE THAT DESIRETH LIFE, AND LOVETH MANY DAYS, THAT HE MAY SEE GOOD? KEEP THY TONGUE FROM EVIL, AND THY LIPS FROM SPEAKING GUILE. DEPART FROM EVIL, AND DO GOOD; SEEK PEACE, AND PURSUE IT. THE EYES OF THE LORD ARE UPON THE RIGHTEOUS, AND HIS EARS ARE OPEN UNTO THEIR CRY. THE FACE OF THE LORD IS AGAINST THEM THAT DO EVIL, TO CUT OFF THE REMEMBRANCE OF THEM FROM THE EARTH".

Therefore if the Scripture is 100% True, how would I explain the saying of many that says before they got Saved, and some will say while they are still a Sinner, they Prayed to God many times and God Delivered them from their troubles. This is the Interpretation of what is said. Man can never be God, nor can man fully understand The Mind of God. It is already Observed and Fixed in The Mind of God from the Foundation of life itself, who it is that would be a Believer; who it will be that will Surrender their lives to God even if it takes a long time for it to happen, God Knows that it will happen and must happen. God Knows who it is that will give Him a Clean Sacrifice, even before that person even know for themselves what they will be doing for The Glory and The Manifestation of God's Kingdom.

Therefore while it is that a person that was in Sin, find themselves with their backs against the wall, and their only help is to cry out to God; if it is already Destined that such a person should be Saved, with the main Ingredience that they will Surrender to Repentance, which means that such a person will Turn, will Change their lifestyle from that of Sin to that of God's Way; then by accepting The Requirements of God, that Faith of that Individual would have created for them a Spiritual key, that will Unlock the Mercy Door of God's Order, to ensure that such an individual receive of the access to Pray a Prayer with the Ingredience of Repentance, that will Force God to first Hear, then to See such a Sinner in Sin, and then Choose to Grant the Deliverance that is needed, even though the time for that person to fully surrender is not fully at hand. The Bible made mention in The Book of Isaiah Chapter 55:8&9.

"FOR MY THOUGHTS ARE NOT YOUR THOUGHTS, NEITHER ARE YOUR WAYS MY WAYS, SAITH THE LORD. FOR AS THE HEAVENS ARE HIGHER THAT THE EARTH, SO ARE MY WAYS HIGHER THAN YOUR WAYS, AND MY THOUGHTS THAN YOUR THOUGHTS".

There is a lot of things in this life that we will not be able to explain, unless God The Creator of all things Reveals The Mystery of what is to be Revealed. Only those who have been given the Access by God to Receive of His God Head, only those Saints will be able to express to some level the Understanding of what God is Doing. Man always work in the Physical, but God Ways are Perfected and can only be found in The Spiritual; and to find God's Way, a Child of God has to Dig Deep in God Words; because God's Way is not found on the surface, but in the Dark Lonely Hole of Uncertainty.

Now here is One Question I wish to ask my Readers to ask themselves: "AM I A REPENTED BAPTIZED BELIEVER?" if not, then What Am I? God's Blessing; Pastor Lerone Dinnall.

REPENTANCE.

FREE WILL

Message # 9   **Date started July 1, 2016.**
Date finished July 1, 2016.

HOW GREAT, WONDERFUL AND Marvelous is our God; I Greet you all the Family of God, in the Mighty Name of Jesus Christ our Soon Coming King. Here we have a Topic that I have been longing to explore; not only for you my Readers but for my own benefit, to discover what the Lord is going to Reveal through this Message for my life and also for your life. I look on this Topic has being very important because it speaks to everything we do as a Child of God; therefore I took the liberty to look for the meaning of the word FREE WILL. According to the Webster's Dictionary it states: Free and independent choice; voluntary decision. The dictionary also says that Free Will is indeed a Doctrine which expresses that the conduct of human beings expresses personal choice, and is not simply determined by physical or divine forces. The main thing that I would want us to understand, from the explanation of the dictionary, is the word that says CHOICE. The meaning of this word says: An act or instance of choosing; selection. The right; power; or opportunity to choose; option.

My only prayer is that when we have gone through this Topic, we would have become better Christians; knowing more clearly that power is ours to choose; but unwise decision will always lead us to fall. I'm not completely certain if the word FREE WILL is in the Bible without the term of an Offering or Sacrifice; but I'm completely certain that God Gave to His People always the opportunity to choose for themselves. There can be said that every event that took place in the Bible, that People; City; Nation or Country is going to be Destroyed; God Brings forth a WARNING, of what is about to happen, thus leaving that Kingdom; Nation or Person with a Choice to make; weather to continue doing what they are doing or to turn to God by Repenting of their Sin. There will be many that will say, that the one event that took place, which brings forth this word called FREE WILL; would have been that which happen to Adam and Eve in the Garden. I did a lot of thinking on this Topic, therefore letting me understand a piece what is in the Mind of God concerning this Topic, by the Revelation of God. This is what the Lord Explain to me: Being God, the first thing we have got to understand is, for God; all His Actions are considered Good and Perfect. It is demonstrated in the Bible when God was Creating the Heaven and the Earth. Genesis 1:31. Says.

"AND GOD SAW EVERYTHING THAT HE HAD MADE, AND BEHOLD, IT WAS VERY GOOD".

My first point to bring in your understanding is that, everything that God the Father of the Universe Do; He Does it with Perfect Intention, that it will always be Good and nothing else. I know that many will say that God also Destroys; there is a difference, God Destroys to Bring forth Good. The next point is a question that I would like you to ask yourself, so that I can answer that question. This is the question: If God Made everything Perfect, and with a Good Intention; how is it that the earth; people of the earth are in the position that they are now in; God made it Very Good; how is it now polluted and corrupt? Before I answer the question, let me say this; many of us are going to look on the obvious, and we are going to say that it was the Sin that Adam and Eve committed, that caused all this to happen. But can we but look closer to identify that there was a Seed that was already sown that caused the outcome of what took place; and that seed is the seed of the Serpent; which is the Devil and Lucifer. We must identify also that after Adam and Eve Sinned; their Sin was not a surprise to God; because after realizing that, they had indeed committed the Sin that He Warned them not to commit. The Lord then Immediately Showed by Manifesting why He is The Alpha and The Omega. He began to put things in order; to signify that His Will must be done. To now answer the question that I asked you to ask yourself. The Lord Allowed me to realize, that because God is always Seeking to Do all that He is Doing with Perfect Intentions; and the final Thought of God is Kingdom Building. Therefore because God is Desirous of a Kingdom; of which all those who are a part of His Kingdom, will enjoy the Liberty of being God's Chosen People; thus we will have all right to eat of the TREE OF LIFE; therefore allowing that person which chooses to Serve God to live Forever.

With all this in view, in The Mind of God; The Lord Allowed me to Understand that the only way He can Truly Judge who is worthy to receive and Inherit this Kingdom to Live Forever, is to Create a Screening through Wisdom known as FREE WILL. By Free Will no one can pretend their way into Heaven. The Lord Established His Kingdom in Heaven; there arose a spirit of ENVY from Lucifer; at that time was known as the Bright and Morning Star. This Lucifer ENVIED GOD'S KINGDOM; he ENVIED GOD'S GLORY; this Seed of ENVY consumed his Mind and filled his heart to have the Intention of wanting to carry out his desire. This Lucifer that was in Heaven; is the Bad Seed we spoke about. This is the Bad Seed that came and Corrupted the Mind of Eve; that cause Adam also to be in Sin. This Seed of ENVY filled the eyes of Adam and Eve, causing them to fail the Test of Free Will. Thus proving to God that they were not Worthy of the Glory He had Bestow upon them. So is it with us, we are living this Christian life; we must be aware of the TEST; which is known as FREE WILL; that will Demonstrate to God that we are indeed a Vessel that is Worthy of all His Blessings that is to come upon us.

Have a look on everyone that you recognize to be a Child of God, and also those who are not Serving God. YES! Each and every one has got to face the TEST, which is known as FREE WILL; not one will escape. There will be many people that will say that, if they were in the position that Adam and Eve was in; they would have not Sin. Truth be told, if we were in the position, we would have done the exact same thing. Reason being; the Seed of ENVY. Ask yourself why in the New Jerusalem, there will be no Sin! The reason why there is no Sin is because God would have then Destroyed all Evidence of Sin. Therefore there can be no more evidence of Sin to corrupt or even seek to tempt anyone to commit Sin. Thus Establishing God's Prefect Kingdom; a Kingdom that is free from all influence of Sin. No more Seed of Envy that brought forth the First Sin; No more Lucifer and his angels; no more Worker of Iniquity; no more Temptation; no more Trials; no more TEST. No more, no more; Praise the Lord No More, Amen. How Great, Wonderful and Marvelous is Our God. From the Servant of God, my prayer for us all is that we will be Mindful of the TEST; that we can make it into God's Kingdom together; knowing that it is only by His Will were able to be found Worthy to pass the Test. I hope this Message was a Blessing to you; I know it is for me; REMAIN SAVED. Pastor Lerone Dinnall.

FREE WILL

COVENANTS;
COMMANDMENTS; VOWS

Message # 72   Date Started May 22, 2017
                                 Date Finalized May 29, 2017.

DEUTERONOMY CHAPTER 29:29. "THE SECRET THINGS BELONG UNTO THE LORD OUR GOD: BUT THOSE THINGS WHICH ARE REVEALED BELONG UNTO US AND TO OUR CHILDREN FOR EVER, THAT WE MAY DO ALL THE WORDS OF THIS LAW".

DEUTERONOMY CHAPTER 4:23-28. "TAKE HEED UNTO YOURSELVES, LEST YE FORGET THE COVENANT OF THE LORD YOUR GOD, WHICH HE MADE WITH YOU, AND MAKE YOU A GRAVEN IMAGE, OR THE LIKENESS OF ANYTHING, WHICH THE LORD THY GOD HATH FORBIDDEN THEE. FOR THE LORD THY GOD IS A CONSUMING FIRE, EVEN A JEALOUS GOD. WHEN THOU SHALT BEGET CHILDREN, AND YE SHALL HAVE REMAINED LONG IN THE LAND, AND SHALL CORRUPT YOURSELVES, AND MAKE A GRAVEN IMAGE, OR THE LIKENESS OF ANYTHING, AND SHALL DO EVIL IN THE SIGHT OF THE LORD THY GOD, TO PROVOKE HIM

TO ANGER: I CALL HEAVEN AND EARTH TO WITNESS AGAINST YOU THIS DAY, THAT YE SHALL SOON UTTERLY PERISH FROM OFF THE LAND WHEREUNTO YE GO OVER JORDON TO POSSESS IT; YE SHALL NOT PROLONG YOUR DAYS UPON IT, BUT SHALL UTTERLY BE DESTROYED. AND THE LORD SHALL SCATTER YOU AMONG THE NATIONS, AND YE SHALL BE LEFT FEW IN NUMBER AMONG THE HEATHEN, WHITHER THE LORD SHALL LEAD YOU. AND THERE YE SHALL SERVE GODS, THE WORK OF MEN'S HANDS, WOOD AND STONE, WHICH NEITHER SEE, NOR HEAR, NOR EAT, NOR SMELL".

DEUTERONOMY CHAPTER 30:15-20. "SEE, I HAVE SET BEFORE THEE THIS DAY LIFE AND GOOD, AND DEATH AND EVIL; IN THAT I COMMAND THEE THIS DAY TO LOVE THE LORD THY GOD, TO WALK IN HIS WAYS, AND TO KEEP HIS COMMANDMENTS AND HIS STATUES AND HIS JUDGMENTS, THAT THOU MAYEST LIVE AND MULTIPLY: AND THE LORD THY GOD SHALL BLESS THEE IN THE LAND WHITHER THOU GOEST TO POSSESS IT. BUT IF THINE HEART TURN AWAY, SO THAT THOU WILT NOT HEAR, BUT SHALT BE DRAWN AWAY, AND WORSHIP OTHER GODS, AND SERVE THEM; I DENOUNCE UNTO YOU THIS DAY, THAT YE SHALL SURELY PERISH, AND THAT YE SHALL NOT PROLONG YOUR DAYS UPON THE LAND, WHITHER THOU PASSEST OVER JORDON TO POSSESS IT. I CALL HEAVEN AND EARTH TO RECORD THIS DAY AGAINST YOU, THAT I HAVE SET BEFORE YOU LIFE AND DEATH, BLESSING AND CURSING: THEREFORE CHOOSE LIFE, THAT BOTH THOU AND THY SEED MAY LIVE: THAT THOU MAYEST LOVE THE LORD THY GOD, AND THAT THOU MAYEST OBEY HIS VOICE, AND THAT THOU MAYEST CLEAVE UNTO HIM: FOR HE IS THY LIFE, AND THE LENGTH OF THY DAYS: THAT THOU MAYEST DWELL IN THE LAND WHICH THE LORD SWARE UNTO THY FATHERS, TO ABRAHAM, TO ISAAC, AND TO JACOB, TO GIVE THEM".

I Give Honour, Praise and find it to be my Desire to always give Glory to The God of the Universe Jesus Christ the Lamb of God. Happy am I to again be in this position of writing another Message for God's People; Glad am I no stranger to the Fellowship of the

Mystery of the Knowledge of God. We must become desirous to Understand in order to be Knowledgeable, so that we can apply the use of Wisdom concerning the significance surrounding the meaning of the words Covenant; Commandment and Vows towards our daily lives of walking this Christian path way; knowing that The Bible made mention to us, that the only way we can be destroyed, is for a lack of Knowledge. Hosea Chapter 4:6. Let us first seek to establish some of the Dictionary's meaning for the words we are seeking to understand.

COVENANT: The Webster's Dictionary state that this is an agreement usually formal, between two or more persons to do or not to do something specified.

COMMANDMENT: This word is coming from the word Command which is its foundation meaning being: To direct with specific authority; a demand or specific requirement such as the Ten Commandments in the Bible.

VOW: A Solemn promise, pledge, or personal commitment such as a Marriage Vow; a solemn pledge made to a deity or a saint committing oneself to an act, service, or condition; usually made through a declaration by the confession of the mouth to do what is Promised or Vowed.

Covenants and Commandments are laws and requirement that comes from God to man, that man should seek to understand to walk in the Statues of the Almighty God, thus preserving the life and the Relationship that God Has Established between Himself and Mankind. Commandment is considered a must, as disobedience to God's Commandment will result in death; Covenant on the other hand is a contract between a Servant and God, in which God Request for a specific type of Relationship between Himself and that Servant, and also the Generation of that Servant, in which that specific Covenant maybe different from other Servants Relationship with God, but God has Chosen Servants for different duties to be performed in His House, thus it requires a different Discipline and Relationship with God, which reflect a Specific Covenant between that Servant and

God. An Example of a Servant that has a Covenant with God is that of a Priest and his Generation for the Service of God in the House of God. Vows is manufactured by man to God, by which a Servant of God Vows to accomplish a specific task, of which, I must warn that the Bible explain that it is better not to Vow than to Vow; because once a Servant of God chooses to Vow before God, that Vow will now have to be fulfilled. I explained this Topic unto the Saints that are a part of my Assembly, and my Advice to them concerning Vows, is not to Vow, unless you have put yourself in the position that you have 90% - 100% in your possession, that which you are going to Vow; because the Bible said that we are looked on as a Fool in God's Eye if we cannot fulfill what we say we have Vowed. Furthermore, it is important to know that whenever a Child of God makes a Vow; the devil the hater of everything that is good, realizes that with every Vow that a Child of God is able to accomplish, this will then bring forth a New and Fresh Release of God's Anointing of Favors upon that Servant's life; therefore it will now be his duty to do everything in his power, just to prevent that Servant from fulfilling that which He / She has Vowed that they will perform for God. Another way to look on it, is that everything we Vow has to be Tested; because every successful Vow brings forth a Divine Release of Favors from God, therefore remember that the Word of God Stands forever, and it is the same Word that is going to try you, by putting what you have Vowed on God's Measuring Scale; and if it is measured that your Vow has the Ingredience of that which Stands forever, which is The Word of God, then without doubt, God Will Enable that Servant to fulfill that which they have Vowed, because that which is Vowed would have given God Pleasure.

Is it fair for me to say that all Saints that are Serving God to the best of their ability, is likely to become those Saints by which the Word of God Says: "HE THAT DWELLETH IN THE SECRET PLACE OF THE MOST HIGH SHALL ABIDE UNDER THE SHADOW OF THE ALMIGHTY". Psalms 91:1. And I think that suggestion is true.

Driving one day, The Spirit of The Lord Asked me to take a look at certain individuals, that were on the road, not being in a good

Mind, and in an attitude of being what a normal person should be doing and behaving; and while looking to understand what it is that The Lord would have me to Understand from what He has Asked me to look on; The Voice of The Lord then Said:

"WHAT DO YOU THINK HAPPENED THAT CAUSED SUCH AN INDIVIDUAL TO BE IN THE POSITION THAT THEY ARE CURRENTLY WALKING IN, AND WHAT HAS NOW BECOME THEIR WHOLE LIFE AND FUTURE?"

Just like Ezekiel when The Lord Asked him if he taught these dry bones could live; Ezekiel response was: "THOU KNOWEST LORD". My response to the Question that was asked, was I don't know why those individuals are now walking and living in the condition that they are now in. The Lord Response was to let me know that for many that we have seen on the road suffering, begging, diseased plagued, handicap in the their situation; it was by a result of such a person not being able to keep God's Covenant; to keep God's Commandments; to keep a Vow that they have made between themselves and God. And by this action such a person is put in a position as this firstly, to identify if that person would see themselves, Repent of the wrongs which they have done, and then seek to again to establish the Covenant; Commandments; and Vows which they have made between themselves and The Almighty God. And if this person refuses to acknowledge that they have Sinned and is in need of restoration, then that person will remain in the state that they are now in, and that state of life will then carry them to the Grave. Upon recognizing the Revelation of this Mystery, I then realize that there is truly no respect of person with God. I then realize that what The Lord was Allowing me to understand was indeed in The Bible. Did not King Nebuchadnezzar boast himself against the Power of God and found himself soon after to become the likeness of an Animal; and it was not until he discovered that he was but just a man, that there was only one True Power, that being the Authority and the Power that comes from God. Then after he recognize God to be The All Power God; he was restored to his original place in life to be the king of Babylon. Daniel Chapter 4. There is also a Story in The

Book of 2 Chronicles Chapter 33. Regarding Manasseh the son of Hezekiah. Manasseh did and did and continue to do evil in the sight of The Lord, and he caused all Israel to Sin against God, and even when The Lord Spoke to him and his people, he did not hearken; this action by Manasseh provoked The Lord to Anger, in that The Lord Brought upon them the captains of the host of the king of Assyria, which took Manasseh among the thorns, and bound him with fetters, and carried him to Babylon. The Bible said in verse 12&13.

"AND WHEN HE WAS IN AFFLICTION, HE BESOUGHT THE LORD HIS GOD, AND HUMBLED HIMSELF GREATLY BEFORE THE GOD OF HIS FATHERS, AND PRAYED UNTO HIM: AND HE WAS INTREATED OF HIM, AND HEARD HIS SUPPLICATION, AND BROUGHT HIM AGAIN TO JERUSALEM INTO HIS KINGDOM. THEN MANASSEH KNEW THAT THE LORD HE WAS GOD".

There must also be the understanding that, not only are we in danger of breaking the Covenants; Commandments and Vows; but also it is a known Fact, that whoever it is that seeks to cause a Saint of God that is seeking their utmost best to keep God's Covenant; Commandment and Vows; that soul will automatically become a danger of the consequences that surrounds a person that has willfully broken the Rules and the Guidelines of The Almighty God. St Matthew Chapter 18:6&7. Says:

"BUT WHOSO SHALL OFFEND ONE OF THESE LITTLE ONES WHICH BELIEVE IN ME, IT WERE BETTER FOR HIM THAT A MILLSTONE WERE HANGED ABOUT HIS NECK, AND THAT HE WERE DROWNED IN THE DEPTH OF THE SEA. WOE UNTO THE WORLD BECAUSE OF OFFENCES! FOR IT MUST NEEDS BE THAT OFFENCES COME; BUT WOE TO THAT MAN BY WHOM THE OFFENCE COMETH!"

Jonah was such a person that suffered the consequences of not doing what the Lord Commanded him to fulfill; of which when he saw himself and Repented and Prayed to The God of Heaven inside the fish belly, The Lord heard his Prayer, and spoke to the fish, and the fish vomited out Jonah upon the dry land; thereafter the journey to Nineveh should have taken Jonah three (3) days, but Jonah now recognizing that the Business of The King require an immediate haste, he entered Nineveh a day's journey. Jonah Chapter 1- Chapter 3. There is no doubt that if Jonah decided not to Repent and prayed before God, he would have continued in the same situation that he was in, being in the fish belly until he died. But because of his Repentance, this action caused God to Release the punishment of which he suffered for Disobedience.

Cain the brother of Abel the sons of Adam and Eve, this Same Cain was Cursed by God, and not only him but all his descendants was marked by the Curse that God had Pronounce upon their Father Cain. A curse spoken by the mouth of Cain, was such that he said: "MY PUNISHMENT IS GREATER THAN I CAN BEAR". And even when Cain thought that death by anyone who see him shall be his escape from the curse; The Lord said unto him in verse 15 of Genesis Chapter 4:

"AND THE LORD SAID UNTO HIM, THEREFORE WHOSOEVER SLAYETH CAIN, VENGEANCE SHALL BE TAKEN ON HIM SEVENFOLD. AND THE LORD SET A MARK UPON CAIN, LEST ANY FINDING HIM SHOULD KILL HIM".

So is it for those in the world now, that have willfully broken the Covenants, Commandments and Vows of God; God has Placed a Mark over their ways and their lives; that unless that person sees themselves to Repent of the wrongs which they have committed, they will remain in the position that God has Placed them to walk in until they have Learnt; and if they will not come to the understanding of their wrongs, then they will die in their sins.

In The Book of Acts Chapter 9. Brother Paul who was first known as Saul, found himself on the wrong side of God, when he by ignorance was seeking to imprison, to punish and also to kill if necessary those who call upon the Name of The Lord Jesus Christ. Now this is an example of those who seek to fight against those who are seeking to keep the Covenants, Commandments and Vows of God. Verse 3-7 says:

"AND AS HE JOURNEYED, HE CAME NEAR DAMASCUS: AND SUDDENLY THERE SHINED ROUND ABOUT HIM A LIGHT

FROM HEAVEN: AND HE FELL TO THE EARTH, AND HEARD A VOICE SAYING UNTO HIM, SAUL, SAUL, WHY PERSECUTES THOU ME? AND HE SAID, WHO ART THOU, LORD? AND THE LORD SAID, I AM JESUS WHOM THOU PERSECUTES: IT IS HARD FOR THEE TO KICK AGAINST THE PRICKS. AND HE TREMBLING AND ASTONISHED SAID, LORD, WHAT WILT THOU HAVE ME TO DO? AND THE LORD SAID UNTO HIM, ARISE, AND GO INTO THE CITY, AND IT SHALL BE TOLD THEE WHAT THOU MUST DO. AND THE MEN WHICH JOURNEYED WITH HIM STOOD SPEECHLESS, HEARING A VOICE, BUT SEEING NO MAN".

Lord help your Servants to keep your Covenants; Commandments and Vows. I Give Honour and Praise to The Saviour of Mankind Jesus Christ The Lamb of God. Pastor Lerone Dinnall.

COVENANTS; COMMANDMENTS; VOWS.

COMPLETING YOUR CIRCLE

Message # 3   Date Started July 2, 2016
                                Date Finalized July 18, 2016.

I AM THE GOD OF Abraham; I AM The GOD OF Isaac; I AM The GOD OF Israel. I started off this Message in this particular fashion, to make known Who God Is. That whatever God Is; whatever God Was; whatever God Is, in the future; this is one event that remains sure; God must be Revealed in those who Serve Him with the whole Heart; Mind and Soul to be The FIRST. God was Revealed to Moses in a Burning Bush of which He Spoke to him; after Moses was desirous to see the Marvelous sight of a bush burning but not consumed.

The Lord Said to Moses: "MOSES, MOSES. AND HE SAID, HERE AM I. THE LORD SAID, DRAW NOT NIGH HITHER: PUT OFF THY SHOES FROM OFF THY FEET, FOR THE PLACE WHEREON THOU STANDEST IS HOLY GROUND".

The Lord Revealed to Moses, when Moses asked God; who shall I say have sent me, when they ask of me that question? The Lord Revealed to Moses One of His Principal Name: I AM THAT I AM: The Lord Said, tell them that The I AM, hath sent you unto them.

One of the main reason why this is important for us all to know in Completing our Circle; is that a Man's Circle will never be completed; unless the Creator that made him; puts the Relationship along with the Revelation in you, that your Circle will be completed. After The Lord Made man in the Garden of Eden; He said it was not good for the man to be alone. Therefore The Lord Created from the man a help meat, which came from the very ribs of the man, after He had put him to sleep. You would have taught that the man was now Completed; but after all these things done for the man; can I tell you the truth; Man was still not Completed.

Question, How can Man be Completed; when that which was given to him, was not a Foundational support to allow him to stand. If at the end of the day; man did not stand; it therefore means that man had failed! Therefore we must now come to the realization that for a man to Complete his Circle; it does not take a woman; or in the case of a woman, a man. But rather, to Complete your circle it takes A Divine Relationship with God The Father, to enable you to keep all that God Has Given to you, to make your Circle Complete. Therefore a young man desiring to be married one day; and one day hoping for children to be added to his future; and most important for those children to have a continuation of their own life. Can I tell you that all that desiring is very good; but The Bible says: "EXCEPT THE LORD BUILD THE HOUSE, THEY LABOUR IN VAIN THAT BUILT IT".

Therefore it brings us to The Foundational FACT; that if a man is truly serious about Completing his Circle; then that man have got to make sure that his life begins with The Foundation of a True Relationship with God The Father; which will bring forth The Revelation to that very man, that once they are standing on God's Word; it therefore means that they are standing on God Himself. And if you find yourself standing on God; how can you even slide, much less to fall. It is God that is going to Give to every man that has a Relationship with Him, The True Revelation of how to Complete his Circle; and then to keep your Circle closed; free from all interference of the Devil. The song writer says; on Christ The Solid Rock I stand; all other ground is sinking sand.

The Bible Said: St Matthew 16:13-20. "UPON THIS ROCK I WILL BUILD MY CHURCH; AND THE GATES OF HELL SHALL NOT PREVAIL AGAINST IT". Upon The Word and belief that Jesus Christ is God; that also brings forth the same Revelation of Jesus Christ Himself Speaking in The Book of Revelation Chapter 1:8. "I AM ALPHA AND OMEGA, THE BEGINNING AND THE ENDING, SAITH THE LORD, WHICH IS, AND WHICH WAS, AND WHICH IS TO COME, THE ALMIGHTY".

I came to the realization of this Topic from God; because I'm now a Pastor; and it is my job to Oversee everything that is of concern to Members of The Church, and to Potential Sons of God. And one of the main desire I find with The Saints, is a clear intention to Complete their Circle. With this in Mind; it is now my responsibility to give clear instruction, as to what needs to be done to ensure that; the process of the Potential Sons of God, is made a little clearer to ensure that the Circle is Completed properly; with a Foundation; with God being The Head of that Foundation.

There is a clear Instruction from The Lord Himself; by making us know, in The Book of Deut. Chapter 6. Verses 4 and 5. Reveals to us that The Lord is ONE LORD. And one of the foundational duties that every Child of God needs to perform, is to love The Lord our God, with all our heart; and with all our soul; and with all our might. The one main thing that The Lord Need for us to understand is that in everything GOD COMES FIRST. If God does not come First in your life; it means that; your Circle that you desire to Complete; will not have a proper foundation. What am I saying? This is what I am saying: For those who are not yet Married; you need to know these things; God comes before your Wife and Husband; God comes before your Children; God comes before your Job; God comes before your House and your Cars; God comes before your Mother and your Father; God comes before your Friends; God comes before your Pastor; and most importantly, God comes before You, and all your decisions which you make outside of His Will.

If our Father Adam, had this Foundational Discipline inside him; there would be no way, he would have listen to his wife; and ate of the fruit. He obeyed his wife to bring forth evidence to God, and to us, to let us know that he place the words of his wife above The Word of God. The Bible Said that thou shalt have no other gods beside me; because I The Lord thy God is a Jealous God. In a nut shell; whatever you put before God; God is going to Destroy it; because God will never take second place in your life; His place is only Reserved for The First and The Best. Second place is for you and your spouse; but First Place belongs only to God. Therefore in desiring to Complete your Circle; if you choose a partner that does not have any foundational value of God inside of him or her; it therefore means that you will never be able to allow that Circle to be Completed; because it takes God to Complete the Circle for you.

The Bible Said that we should: "SEEK YE FIRST THE KINGDOM OF GOD, AND HIS RIGHTEOUSNESS; AND ALL THESE THINGS SHALL BE ADDED UNTO YOU". One of the main reason why we fail so miserable, is because we do not study how not to fail. And while studying how not to fail; you'll then realize that the only way you are sure not to fail; is to have The God of All Ages at The Head of everything that you do.

Proverbs 3:5-6. Says: "Trust in the Lord with all thine heart; and lean not unto thine own understanding. In all thy ways acknowledge Him, and He will direct thy paths".

What I want us all to realize and to understand; is that Man was never made to lead and to direct his own pathway. Man was made in The Image of God, to replicate what God Desire on earth should be in the lives of mankind. Man was only made; and his true purpose only being to do what God Need for him to do. The Bible said, God Made man in His own Image; after His Likeness. If God Wanted man to do his own will; He would have made him in a different being to fulfill a different purpose, but still this would also establish God's Purpose. Do you know what God is waiting for in our lives? God is waiting for a TRUE SURRENDER; not only from Sinners, but from those of us, who call ourselves Christians; and is just wearing a title that we think we have earned, because we went down in water Baptism. Truth be told; being a Christian is a Title you earn by Surrendering to God's

Will; and doing all that God Command us to Do. Therefore becoming A Christian Requires a Continual Work; to live up. If you have not yet realized that in your life; then it is a certain; your Circle will not be Completed. The Circle is not Completed because you choose for yourself anyone that you desire. **BUT THE CIRCLE IS COMPLETED BECAUSE YOU CHOOSE WHO GOD NEEDED YOU TO CHOOSE. THE CIRCLE IS COMPLETED BECAUSE YOU CHOOSE GOD'S WILL AND REFLECTION.**

There is one Sad fact; this is it, not everyone will be able to Complete their Circle; because not everyone is willing to do and to choose who God Ask of them to Choose. Your life people of God, is only made and design for God's Glory; and only for His Purpose. If your life is not Pleasing The Almighty God; then your life has immediately become a waste; good for nothing else but to be burnt. If you truly want to know what Obedience look like; have a look on The Book of Hosea. This was a Prophet that understood that he was but a Servant made to perform only what God Needed him to Perform. The Lord Told Hosea the Prophet, His Servant to marry a harlot; and if this wasn't bad enough; The Lord Told him to love her, and to have children with the Harlot. And if this wasn't bad enough, The Lord Foretold Hosea that the harlot who he is to marry was going to play the harlot with him; but he must receive her back into his house and never stop loving her. Can I tell you that because Hosea was a Servant, and a Child of God; he Obeyed God's Word. He never once asked God what he was Doing; because he knew that his job was only to do what God Needed him to Do.

How many of us; if The Lord would Ask us right now, to do something out of character; suppose The Lord Told you to look on the young brother, that just one year got saved, but he has not yet started to work; suppose The Lord Said: Sister Mary; that brother right there is your husband to Complete your Circle; you seeing the brother start to look on all the negatives:

"HE DOESN'T LOOK GOOD; HE DRESSES VERY POOR; YOU DOUBTED BECAUSE YOU'LL HAVE TO TAKE ON MOST OF THE RESPONSIBILITY TO MAKE THE MARRIAGE WORK".

Hosea did not doubt; he wasn't displeased; he Obeyed God, because that harlot was his Circle being Completed. Mankind; human being; Servant of The Living GOD; needs to understand that we are but Tools in The Hands of God; to be Used for His Purpose and for His Glory to come from us. If you're Serving God and His True Purpose and Glory is not coming from you; then you need to watch it; because there is someone in line, just waiting and dying to do for God, what He would have them to Do. If you do not Obey God, to take the young brother to be your Husband; or to take that sister to be your Wife; then, don't worry, God is not short of male or female who are not willing to do for Him what He desire for them to Do.

In Completing your Circle, you got to understand that many times we miss the opportunity; and that gift, that should be ours; is now in the possession of someone who did not doubt, but moved in faith. In Completing your Circle; you need to understand that it can only be done by faith; your Husband and your Wife is not going to fall from Heaven. Your partner for life is in no way going to be perfect. This is where a lot of saints are misguided; we believe that when we meet our partner, the stars are going to shine a little brighter; we believe that he or she is going to have all the money to take care of us; we believe that everyone will be in agreement with that person which God Has Given to you; we believe that he or she is going to be well Educated, or well Dressed; and by these details; we allow that which God Has Destined for us, to be the blessing for someone else; because you Rejected what God Gave.

I have found out that one of the biggest problem that God Has with His People, is a word that is called TRUST. Some of us belief, is that you've got to get the approval of fifty people to tell you that the particular person is Chosen by God to Complete your Circle. When all it really takes is The Whisper of The Voice of God Giving you The Confirmation that this is, His Will Being Done. Here we have a twist to this message; because I am of the belief that everyone who has found themselves in the position to Complete their Circle, is actually Saints that are Serving God; and if you are Serving God; it simply means that you're Hearing from God; therefore you can tell the difference between The Voice of God, and the voice of vanity.

If it is that you have not yet known how to tell the difference between the voices; let me give you three (3) clue of what to look out for.

1. The Voice of God must Reflect what The Word of God Says. Therefore to know The Voice of God; you have got to know what The Word of God Says. If you do not know the Word; then you leave yourself open to be fooled by every other voice of vanity.

2. When The Lord Speaks it brings forth A Revelation within your own soul to Confirm that The Lord Has Spoken. This cannot be mistaken; The Bible Said that the disciple said; did not our Hearts burn within us when He Spake to us The Word of God.

3. When The Lord Speaks, He Opens the eyes of the person He is Speaking to. Therefore you will see what The Lord is Saying.

I am very careful of what these Messages are saying to ensure that these words are actually Revelations coming from God unto His People. When I look on my life; I got to realize that I have children that are Heritage for God's Glory; and I have got to ensure that these children while growing, has the proper Instruction to follow, to ensure that they will be directed in the right manner. Things that I struggle with being a child growing in God; I'm now happy that I will be able to give my children Messages Inspired by God, that will enable their Christian life to evolve at a faster paste.

While seeking to Complete your Circle, there is one thing that is certain; and that is THE FIGHT, which is The **TEST**. Do you think that it is going to be easy to Receive what God Has in store for you; with the devil who is the father of everything that is envious; looking at you, receiving Favors and Blessings that he will never be able to receive again! The answer is no; it's not going to be easy. Know this;

every Word that God Speaks from His Mouth, have to pass THE **TEST**.

1. To Pass The Test of your Belief.
2. The Word have to Pass The Test of the Earth; to prove that God did Command whatever you're declaring that He Commanded.
3. To Pass The Test of Principalities and Powers.
4. To Pass The Test of falling Angels; that are set in the atmosphere to delay our Prayers; and not to mention the Devil himself.

It was Daniel that prayed and fasted unto God for three full weeks; The Lord Told him that his prayer was answered immediately; but the adversaries withheld the answer from coming at the time appointed. Daniel Chapter 10. Did not Father Abraham, received Word from God of a promise; that if he obeyed; he would receive! Yes. Abraham believed God; moved by Faith; and walked straight into his TEST.

The Bible Said that after Abraham left his people and his land; the first Test was the **TEST OF** BELIEF that Abraham had to have in order to move by Faith.

The next Test was a TEST OF FAMINE; that he and his family had to go done into Egypt because the famine was so great.

The next Test was the TEST OF FEAR. Abraham feared so much that he never even remember that The Lord Told him that: "I WILL BLESS THEM THAT BLESS THEE, AND CURSE HIM THAT CURSETH THEE: AND IN THEE SHALL ALL THE FAMILIES OF THE EARTH BE BLESSED". Abraham moved with fear, told Sarah his wife that when they go down to Egypt, she should tell everyone that he was her brother. The Pharaoh being plagued by God, returned Sarah unto Abraham.

The TEST OF ENVY among your own family members was next in line. Every time you sing the song, that says: "I'M NEXT IN LINE FOR MY BLESSING; YOU SHOULD ALSO BE SAYING; I'M

NEXT IN LINE FOR MY TESTING". Because every Blessing comes with its equal share of Testing in order to receive that Blessing. The Bible Said that the herdman of Lot; the nephew of Abraham, disagreed with the herdman of Abraham; that they could not dwell together; they had to separate from each other; with Lot choosing what he taught was the better land; not knowing that the moment he choose the plain that look so beautiful at the time; that plain became a curse; because the Man of blessing was not dwelling there. And Abraham choosing the hills; which became his blessing, because God was with him. It must be noted that after Abraham's separation from Lot; it brought forth a new Revelation of Blessing from God; which could only take place because of Separation. In your test, there will be people and even family members; that you have got to separate yourself from; in order to make your Circle to be Completed.

Abraham then went through the TEST OF GREED, which he passed with flying colours; it was the King of Sodom that offered Abraham gifts of value; that Abraham refused. Abraham said to the King: "I HAVE LIFT UP MINE HAND UNTO THE LORD, THE MOST HIGH GOD, THE POSSESSOR OF HEAVEN AND EARTH, THAT I WILL NOT TAKE FROM A THREAD EVEN TO A SHOELATCHET, AND THAT I WILL NOT TAKE ANYTHING THAT IS THINE, LEST THOU SHOULDEST SAY, I HAVE MADE ABRAHAM RICH". Genesis 14:21-24. Abraham needed everyone to know that His God was Completely Sufficient to meet all that his life could require. Many of us fail this test so often; in not allowing other to know that, your GOD is BIG; BIG; BIG.

After this Abraham went through the TEST OF PATIENCE; which he failed. By this his wife Sarah being barren; requested that her husband would sleep with her maid; in order to bring forth a child that would represent the Promised Seed. This child would grow; and became a threat, to the child that came from the womb of Sarah; which is the Promised Child Isaac. Something that they regret, because they didn't have the Patience to Wait on GOD.

After this came the Test for them to STILL BELIEVE, after all hope was now lost. There was no more evidence that they could still have a child; because they were now well stricken in age; Abraham being ninety and nine, and Sarah being ninety. The Bible said that The Lord sent His Messengers; and ask Abraham:

"IS ANYTHING TOO HARD FOR THE LORD? AT THE TIME APPOINTED I WILL RETURN UNTO THEE, ACCORDING TO THE TIME OF LIFE, AND SARAH SHALL HAVE A SON". Genesis 18:14. One year after The Lord Spoke to Abraham, the promise was fulfilled.

But Abraham Test did not stop there; because Abraham now receive the promise from God; he loved his son Isaac; he loved him so much that he made the best feast for him. By doing this, God brought upon Abraham the ultimate test; which is to PROVE THAT HE FEARED GOD. Because in God's Word, He had to prove that Abraham loved no one more than how he loved GOD; because God is and always is a Jealous GOD. The Bible said that The Lord Told Abraham to offer his promised son for a sacrifice upon Mount Moriah. Many people wonder why Abraham was known as the Father of Faith; and also is A FRIEND OF GOD. This was why: Abraham upon hearing the request that God asked him to perform; did not even stop to think; or even stop to discuss what he had to do before his wife; because maybe she would have stopped him; or asked him if he was crazy. The Bible said that Abraham rose up early the morning, and saddled his ass, and took two young men with him along with his son Isacc. The Bible Said upon reaching the mountain he asked the two young men to tarry with the ass; while he and his son go yonder and worship. Before they reached the place where the sacrifice should be offered; Isaac his son asked him; where is the lamb; because he saw the fire and the wood. Abraham replied to him; God will provide Himself a lamb. When they reached the place to offer the sacrifice; Abraham took the promised son; bound him; took the knife and was ready to kill him. The Bible Said that The Angel of The Lord Spoke from Heaven Said:

"ABRAHAM, ABRAHAM, LAY NOT THINE HAND UPON THE LAD, NEITHER DO THOU ANYTHING TO HIM: FOR NOW I KNOW

THAT THOU FEAREST GOD, SEEING THOU HAST NOT WITHHELD THY SON, THINE ONLY SON FROM ME".

The Word and The Promise from God is good, and blessed; but the TEST is there to see if we truly deserve what God Promised. There is a Big comfort for us, that have Received God's Word; whenever God Speaks; He then Sow a seed in your soul, that will forever be with you; as long as you water that seed, it will grow; that no matter what Test comes your way; you will in the Test be able to rise above the Test. God who Speaks to you also Said: Isaiah 46:9-10.

"REMEMBERING THE FORMER THINGS OF OLD: FOR I AM GOD, AND THERE IS NONE ELSE; I AM GOD, AND THERE IS NONE LIKE ME. DECLARING THE END FROM THE BEGINNING, AND FROM ANCIENT TIMES THE THINGS THAT ARE NOT YET DONE, SAYING, MY COUNSEL SHALL STAND, AND I WILL DO ALL MY PLEASURE".

Before God Spoke to you; He already Knows that He is ABLE to Help you to pass every Test.

It is important also to note that, The Test of your life may not come in the same pattern that it came with for Abraham. Your Test may be of some different order; because not everyone has the same weakness; but you can be very sure that everyone has a weakness that they are working on; or have worked on, in order to be an Overcomer. It is also important to know that when God Gives you a Gift to Complete your Circle; do everything that is in your power to ensure that you take the very best care of that which God has Given to you. You don't want to be like the servant that received the one talent; and went and buried that talent. For those who are Married; and you know that God is your True Foundation; and not a man or a woman: Treat I pray, that Marriage Relationship as the one talent that God has Given to you to work on it, that it may Multiply. For those who are not yet Married; when the time has come, that God Gives you the privilege of that Gift; please may sure that you look at that Gift as the very best Gift, that God could ever Give to you. You're not going to Worship or to Praise that Gift; you're instead going to do your very best to take care of that Gift; and let God know that you appreciate the Gift that He has Given to you.

Next; when you have received your Gift, to Complete your Circle; do not allow anyone to INTERFERE with your Circle; especially those who do not have a Circle for themselves. No matter what instruction they give to you; it is only given to destroy what God Has Given to you. Can a man speak about the Trial of a Marriage; if he had not been in a Marriage! Can he speak about the Pain and the Responsibilities faced; if he did not experience it for himself! With all the advice that a person will give to you; do they know the level of Discipline you have to achieve, in order to REMAIN MARRIED? Think; if God was Pleased with them; would He not have Given them also A Gift to Complete their Circle? Therefore whatever you are facing in your Circle; for a person that is Married like yourself; to give you an advice, that person will only have a word of Encouragement to give to you; because they will now know that it take God to keep the Circle Unbroken. It is your Circle; in which way you desire to treat it; you cannot be surprise at the fruits that bear from it; because whatever a man sow; that shall he reap.

I would like very much to speak to my Readers concerning the VOW. Now according to the Webster's Dictionary, the word Vow means: A Solemn Promise; Pledge; or Personal commitment. **AN EARNEST DECLARATION MADE BY SOMEONE WHO IS SOBER AND OF THE FULL KNOWLEDGE AND UNDERSTANDING OF WHAT THEY ARE VOWING TO PERFORM.** The word Vow means that you the person that have Vowed, is going to ACT in all capacity of your life to make sure that this Vow is kept; No Excuse. For those who are members of The Church of Jesus Christ Fellowship Family; I call upon you to take a look at your Certificate you received, when you got Baptized. The Certificate is called; Reminder of your Vows to God. On this Certificate, it is clearly explained, by the giving of Scripture to enlighten every believer of their responsibilities of being A Child of God. These Scripture are as follows: Deut. 23:21-23. Numbers 30:1-4. Ecc. 5:1-6. Ps. 50:14. Ps. 66:13&14. Ps. 76:11. With these Scriptures you will clearly identify that Vows are not to be taken LIGHTLY. You cannot tell The Lord that, you made a mistake; or that you are sorry. God is Expecting you to fulfill your Vows.

Let's take a look at some of The Vows we make before God to Complete that Circle of our lives.

1. I VOW to Love my partner as long as we both shall live:
2. I VOW to be with my partner for better or for WORSE. I made sure I bolded the worse because, we tend to forget about that part; everyone is happy with the better; no complaints; but when things start to get bad; for many people it's a sign to run.
3. I VOW to be with my partner in SICKNESS and in HEALTH; for RICH or for POOR; FORSAKING ALL OTHERS; Till death do us part.

That's the VOW! For those who are looking to Complete your Circle; are you Truly ready for this??? Don't look on The Pastor; he's only God's Tool; it is your Personal FREE WILL that you choose to VOW. Let me tell you the TRUTH: It is God that Design Marriage; He Spoke it into Existence because He Knew it was Possible; But only through Him; and only by Him; Only for His Glory, and for His Purpose.

What I'm really saying is this: If God is not at the Center of your life; and at the center of your spouse life; then truth be told; you have already failed; a mixture for disaster; you just don't know it yet. Married, and don't know God; FAILED: Married and don't believe in God; FAILED. Married, and not depending on God to see you through; FAILED. Married and not Serving God; FAILED. Married, and pretending to others, that your Marriage is working; FAILED; FAILED; FAILED.

It is my job as a Pastor to OPEN your EYES to the Future. The Future and The Circle that have Accepted GOD, has the FOUNDATION, equals VICTORY; the Future and The Circle that have no evidence of God, being the FOUNDATION, will; must; very sure; will result in Failure. And that's the whole truth; and nothing but the truth. NOTE: When God Design Marriage He had one thing in Mind; and that is Children; His Inheritance; not yours.

Therefore for those who are not planning to have children; but desiring to be Married; think again! The last thing you want to happen, is for you to enter a relationship with the wrong intentions. The Bible Said that Marriage is Honorable; and the bed undefiled; but Sinners and Whoremongers God Will Judge. There is A Special Blessing that Proceed from God; for those Couples that have their FOUNDATION to be GOD. It is God's Intension to make every True Couple to become A Generation of RIGHTEOUSNESS. If you're not ready for this calling over your life; then truth be told; you're definitely not ready to Complete your Circle.

Think on these things. For someone that has been Married for five (5) years; I can clearly tell you that Marriage is A BIG TEST. Because every step of the way; you've got to be proving to God; proving to your wife or husband; proving to man; and most importantly, proving to yourself; that the VOWS you've made is real; is true; and you're fully determine; and persuaded that it will work; it must work; with every fiber of your body; soul and might; along with the Help of God; it is going to WORK. Let me share something with you; **IF YOU ARE A CHRISTIAN; AND YOUR FINDING IT DIFFICULT, TO BE FAITHFUL TO GOD. THEN, THE TRUTH IS; WEATHER YOU WANT TO BELIEVE IT OR NOT; YOU WILL NEVER BE FAITHFUL TO YOUR PARTNER; THEREFORE YOU WILL FAIL, FACT.**

For those who are not yet Married; if you need to have A REAL RELATIONSHIP with your Future husband or wife; then take my advice; start to work on your Relationship with GOD. Because one of the number one tools to have in a Relationship is Communication; and if you cannot communicate with God; who is not going to tell anyone that which you told Him; how is it that, you're going to communicate with someone that has faults like yourself. And if it is that you're a person that says: I have no problem communicating with my spouse; but I just can't find the time to speak to The Lord. Be very careful, because you have just put your spouse in the position that God should be Occupying. Therefore the word will fall on you and your spouse, that says:

"DO NOT FORGET ABOUT GOD; LEST THE ANGER OF THE LORD BE KINDLED, AND DESTROY YOU FROM OFF THE FACE OF THE EARTH; FOR I THE LORD THY GOD IS A JEALOUS GOD".

Love your Husbands, and your Wives; and your Children; but make sure that The Love for God; far exceeds, that of your husband and your wife; and your children. Speak to your husband; and your wife; but make sure you speak to God FIRST, and more often. Because God will remove every distraction that comes between Him and His Glory; believe that! You've been WARNED. For those who are seeking to get married and have not yet found your true partner; I know that this is hard. There are times that you will get in a position that you find yourself going out of character, because you want to do everything in your power to try and attract the person you're desiring a relationship with. Therefore upon approaching that special person; you'll find yourself being nervous; not able to communicate as you know that you can; because you're trying so hard to ensure that you impress that special person you're desiring to complete your circle with. I know this for a fact; because that's what happen to me.

But what if, in your seeking, you find that you are the only person that is showing any interest? Then it maybe, and is a great possibility that the person you're seeking to attract, is just not interested. While seeking, it is important to know that; it's not everything that glitter is actual gold; and if it is that it is gold; it's not the gold that is designed for you. That is why, it is important to make sure that you SEEK THE LORD; concerning your Circle; to ensure that it is indeed God that brought forth The Revelation of the person that is to Complete your Circle.

Planning to get married! It therefore means that you have already plan for yourself and for your partner where you're going to live. You've also made sure that, you have put aside some money; to start the new life that you're entering into. It also means that a least one member of this relationship is in a steady job; that will meet the requirement of the expenses that will occur. It would be ideal if both party is working; because there is a saying that goes like this: ONE HAND CANNOT CLAP; IT TAKES TWO HANDS TO CLAP. If no one is working; it therefore means that you're not ready for Marriage. Marriage is Responsibility; Marriage is Hard Work; Marriage takes a lot of MONEY; weather you want to believe it or not. Marriage is not a GAME; it's not something you pick up today and tomorrow you forget that your Married; it is serious business; it not a SHOW or a MOVIE; it's not ACTING; it is BEING and BECOMING what God Needs you to BE; it is REAL.

It is important for you to know that, when you get Married; you're no longer the responsibility of your parents or your guardian; you're now fully responsible for yourself and your spouse; and for all that should come from you both.

The Bible Said: "THEREFORE SHALL A MAN LEAVE HIS FATHER AND HIS MOTHER, AND SHALL CLEAVE UNTO HIS WIFE: AND THEY SHALL BE ONE FLESH". Genesis 2:24.

You will never be Completed as One; if you're still lingering around your parent's home; because their rules will still be Governing your new life. Therefore your Marriage will be influence by a third party.

We are speaking about Completing your Circle; therefore we have to give you every information necessary for you to know what it takes for you to build your NEW LIFE.

RESPONSIBILITIES

For the Man; your job becoming a husband must entail; Loving God, that the expression of that love; will reflect the love that you will have for your wife; if a man does not love God; Ladies, that's a sign that he will never love you. He will pretend to love; but pretend only last for a season. This will result in you spreading that love towards your children to come. A Good Husband will result to be A Good Father; just as it is, A Good Servant will result to be A Good Leader. Being The Head of your Family: There must be an understanding in every relationship, concerning who is going to be the Head; the Leader; the person responsible to make the Final Decision; and that person according to The Bible; is the Man.

Now you have to understand The MIND of GOD; God Designed Marriage for those who will Obey Him; therefore if the Man is not Obeying God; it therefore means that the Man will never be able to lead his own house. Ladies; if you have a problem with the man being the head of your relationship; then you're setting up yourself to have a life time of problem in that same relationship. The Bible Said that wives must be submissive to their husband; which means to be under his rule; but the condition of this act is; only IF, the man is being Submissive to GOD. It therefore means that the ladies / wives need not to worry about their husband leading them; because if God is Leading your husband; there is NO WAY your husband can lead you astray. Ephesians 5:21-29.

One of the main purpose and meaning of a man, is a word that is called STRENGHT and LEADERSHIP. The main meaning and purpose for the Woman is; BEAUTY; SUPPORT and CHILD BEARING. I have a little picture that I purchased from a store; the word of it says: "MEN MAKE HOUSES, WOMEN MAKE HOMES". The meaning of these words state that while the men go out to bring in the earning to build a house for his family; it is the women that allow that house to become a home; somewhere that both she and her husband, along with their children will be happy to dwell in and make Memories.

SECRET: It is the memories that you make with your family, that allow your family to grow and to overcome every challenge; to ensure that your family can make more wonderful memories.

Husbands; always seek to continue to love your wives; you will realize that by doing so; you will unlock all her Beauty; all her Support and will receive a lot of Fruits through child bearing that will enable your joy to be full. The Bible Said:

"HAPPY IS THE MAN THAT HATH HIS QUIVER FULL OF THEM: THEY SHALL NOT BE ASHAMED, BUT THEY SHALL SPEAK WITH THE ENEMIES IN THE GATE". Psalms 127:5.

Wives; be submissive to your husbands; allow him to lead; and if you see that he is not fully capable; that's where you come in; to be supportive. Support him in your Prayers and Fasting; Ask God to equip him with Wisdom; Knowledge and Understanding; for him to be able to make the right decisions to lead the family. Wives; make yourself available; for that time when the decision is made to have children; because the whole purpose of Marriage, is to bring forth your CONTINUATION; which is God's Inheritance. Wives; if you but show to your husband all the Support that he needs; then you will be able to unlock all his Strength; and even the strength that is reserved.

Men; if the woman that you're desiring to marry; if you have not prepared yourself to give it your all; don't even start. Because The Bible Said that men ought to love their wives; as their own bodies. He that loveth his wife, loveth himself. Let me tell you something about Love; If you don't prepare yourself for Marriage; you don't really know love; if you don't do everything in your power to allow your Marriage to work; then you're just another person that is only speaking the word love; but definitely knows not what it means. For preparation for marriage; I would advise everyone to read The Book of 1 Corinthians 13. These Words will allow you to measure up to the Requirements of LOVE.

When you go before The Pastor and before God to exchange your Vows; when you say I DO; that's mainly the mouth that is speaking; it is the life that you will now live; that is what will determine that; that which you Vowed; is what your desiring to live up to become. It's not how pretty you make your Vows to sound; it is how determine you are to ensure that you keep the VOW. You will recall that I'm always saying this: It's not to get The Blessing; it's important to know how to keep The Blessing. For those who are desiring to get Married; if you're not ready to work the HARDEST you've ever worked in your life; don't even bother attempting to get Married; if there is another way to spell Marriage; it would be spelt like this:

"HARD WORK; WHICH EQUALS GREAT REWARDS".

NOTE: Before you got Married; you were responsible for

yourself; or your parents took care of you. Now that you are Married or getting ready to be Married; you are Responsible 100% for your partner; it's no longer mommy or daddy's responsibility to take care of you. You take care of each other; therefore resulting in the fact that; whatever belongs to you; is now going to be the full possession of your spouse. Money; it now as a title of OURS; Car; Home; Children; Furniture; Stocks; Investments; Savings etc. It is now OURS.

For Married Couples; it is important for you to know that, you have got to respect each other; or else the children to come; and those around your Circle, will have no respect for you both. Take Sarah for example; she called Abraham her lord; and there was no one to compare Sarah with; in the eyes of Abraham. Abraham rather to give his life for Sarah rather than to allow one hair of her head to be harmed; but in everything remember to be Temperate; because GOD is A Jealous God; know where your limits are. What is for God; give it to God; what is for your Spouse; give it to them.

There is truly so much more that can be written about this Topic; but we thank God for His Revelation; that will enable us to be aware; to know what to do; in order to Complete our Circle in The Almighty God.

Unto The God of Abraham; Isaac and Israel. From the Servant of GOD; I remain always Your Brother; Your Friend; Your Minister and Pastor.

COMPLETING YOUR CIRCLE.

THE BEST KEPT SECRET.

Message # 39.

Date Started December 8, 2016

Date Finalized December 16, 2016.

I GIVE HONOUR AND Praise and also Magnify The Lord of Host, The King of all kings and The Supreme Ruler of all Universe Jesus Christ. It is truly a privilege for me to be in a position that I can be God's Pen and Mouth Piece, in order to write these Inspiring Messages for God's People to have, in order to help us with the Challenges of this life. I know by looking on this Topic, many will be asking the question: What Secret! Let us begin with the Word of God. Genesis Chapter 2:21-25. Verse 22 explain that God took one of Adam's rib and made a woman, and brought her unto Adam. Verse 23. Explains that Adam having then The Spirit of God which is The Mind of God to be able to see and have the Knowledge of what God Did, even though he was put to sleep. Adam declared and said that this is now bone of my bones, and flesh of my flesh: she shall be called Woman, because she was taken out of Man. Verse 24. Explain and said:

"THEREFORE SHALL A MAN LEAVE HIS FATHER AND HIS

MOTHER, AND SHALL CLEAVE UNTO HIS WIFE: AND THEY SHALL BE ONE FLESH".

Let us seek to explain the Secret that The Lord has for us to be Revealed. The Best kept Secret, what is it? It is the Secret of that which God has Placed in the lives of Men and Women that are Destined to be joined as one, in order to Manifest that which God has in store to be Realized or to be Revealed, which in the end will be the Greatest Manifestation of His Glory. In this World there is always the Manifestation of the Power of the Prince of this world, trying to counteract or to stop that which God has Destined or Decreed for to Happen. Can we remember when Jesus Christ was to be born; the enemy using the vessel of King Herod, to do everything in his power to make sure that the Promised Deliverer was not able to Survive or to Fulfill that which was Destined for Him to Fulfill; but guest what, it didn't and could not work, even though many other male child was killed in the process. Moses when he was born, had to be hidden for three months, and when they could no longer hide him; they made an Ark of Bulrushes, and daubed it with slime and with pitch, and placed Moses in the Ark, because they saw that he was a goodly child. They sent him down the river, where God Provided Pharaoh's Daughter to take the child has her own, the very man that gave the command for every male child to be cast into the river; the Daughter of Pharaoh also employed Moses Mother to take care of her own child without even knowing the Plans of God. Exodus Chapter 1 & 2.

There is one main thing that keeps the enemy puzzled, and that's the thought of Mind that craves to understand, "How is God going to Do what He Said He's going to Do for The Righteous Seed". We got to understand that while the enemy is strong, we have to be born in the knowledge that his strength only applies to this Temporal life, to that which God Permits him to have and to do, to the end will also bring forth Glory to God; beyond this life he has absolutely no power; because beyond this life, there is no need for a Trainer; because we would have already been taught, by knowing what The Characteristics of God are. The Bible Declares that:

"THE SECRET OF THE LORD IS WITH THEM THAT FEAR HIM; AND HE WILL SHEW THEM HIS COVENANT". Psalms 25:14. It is therefore being Manifested in our Minds that, in order to understand the Best kept Secrets of God, it begins with a word and action of Fear for God. The Fear of God will enable us to make decisions that God has Asked us to make, even though it goes beyond everything that we were Trained to accomplish and to fulfill in this life, to move away from Customs; The Fear of God, will allow us to move in a direction Instructed by God, that no manual on Earth has that specific instruction of how to do it in that manner. The Fear of God is Embedded with The Secrets of The Almighty that only The Children of God can receive of that Blessing which is completely hidden from the wiles and wisdom of man and the enemies. It is staggering to realize that the Woman was and is a Secret that is hidden in the very manifestation of that Man that she is Destined for, that even though the enemy tries their very best at least to destroy a Man, to get to the place that the enemy can even attempt to find the Woman to destroy, which brings forth the Future of the Secrets of God; this the enemy will not be able to destroy, if that Man, which is the head of the Family, is able to be in a position that God is The Manifestation of his life. Once it is Revealed that God has Complete Guidance and Authority of this Man's Life, then the Secret which is completely wrapped up in the woman; and for the woman the man, this will never be able to be touch by the cunning devices of the devil. Because this man / woman will have in them The Mind of God, to be able to make the necessary decisions that are needed in order for the Circle of their Marriage to remain Complete. It is always important to remember that the Best Kept Secret has the Manifestation which says: Eyes have not seen, neither can heart comprehend what The Lord has in store for those who Trust Him. It is marvelous to understand that God by His Secret, have Milked Out the Best Ingredience of who we are now, leaving behind the faults of what we have, to Manifest a Greater Production without the weakness of what we now possess, if it is indeed that we have lived up to the Requirements of making sure that we do our jobs by Training our Children in the paths of

Righteousness. We have to understand that the faults we now possess and find difficult to extract from our lives; in The Secret of God that will not be an issue, because God is all about Making things Better; in God's Secret, Creation must continue until Perfection is Attained; and while we know that we are not yet Perfect, here come The Word of God that says: those without us could not be made Perfect.

In Perfection, if you should look closely, you will then realize that everything that is considered to be Perfect must have a Foundation and that Foundation is God, or else Perfection will not and could not be realized. And when we have looked on the Foundation of Perfection, we get to realize that it was Very Rough and Bumpy, had a lot of Steels and Sharp Obstacles, that if we went near, it may cause harm to us if not death. Take for example The Life of Jesus Christ, His Death brought forth Salvation, but have a look at what he had to bear in order for us to be Saved. They Spot in His Face, they Whipped Him, they gave him a Heavy Cross to carry, when He Begged for water, they gave Him Vinegar and Gall; they took a Sword and pierced His Side, they Nailed Him to the Cross and Crucified Him, and these are only a few of the things which was done to The Son of God, The Manifestation of God on Earth; and guest what! **He Had NO SIN**, but yet, this was the price to bring forth Eternal Life. Question: Does Perfection look pretty? Judge for yourself. Realizing and accepting Perfection is not one person's job, but understanding that Perfection can only be achieved together, by The Best Kept Secret that the enemy seeks to destroy each day; this brings forth a joy and comfort to our Mind. It is however no secret to the enemy that his Destruction is EMINENT; because The Lord Revealed to the enemy his final outcome in The Book of Genesis Chapter 3:15. The Secret which shall come from the woman will no doubt bruise thy head, which is the Head of the enemy to bring forth victory. Let us now discussed how important it is to have The Mind of God; because although we are Baptized, and going to Church often, this does not bring us as yet to a Qualified State, that will enable us to Manifest God's Perfect Will according to The Mind of God; Baptism and going to Church often will not be enough to withstand the Rampage of the Enemy. Having The Mind of God is most important, because this life that we are living in, is destined for Ups and Downs, it has on the journey, Good and Bad, don't forget Principalities, Powers, Spiritual Wickedness in High places. This life has Storms, Earthquakes, Tornadoes, Hurricanes, which when they come, and is the Season for them to be revealed, if it is that we are only a Church goer, or only a Baptized Believer, then it is sad to say, that we will not be able to Stand the Turmoil of the Wrath of these Challenges of life that is a must. We can't bypass the Storms of life; it is available for every person that comes on this Earth, and none can escape. There is no get out of Jail card, and there is no Free parking when the Storm comes; this life is not a Game or a Show.

The Bible explains in The Book of St. Matthew Chapter 7:24-29. Which says:

"THEREFORE WHOSOEVER HEARETH THESE SAYING OF MINE, AND DOETH THEM, I WILL LIKEN HIM UNTO A WISE MAN, WHICH BUILT HIS HOUSE UPON A ROCK: AND THE RAIN DESCENDED, AND THE FLOODS CAME, AND THE WINDS BLEW, AND BEAT UPON THAT HOUSE; AND IT FELL NOT: FOR IT WAS FOUNDED UPON A ROCK".

The Scripture went on to say that the person that did not Receive / Accept of the Word of The Lord, was liken unto a foolish man, that when the Challenges of life came, his fall was Very Great. Having The Mind of God is very important because when these challenges arise, it is God that will Reveal His Secrets for us to know how exactly to keep alive when the Season of the Hurricane has come. One of the Main Duties of The Holy Ghost is to be a Comforter, and one of the Purpose while Comforting is to Protect; and that's what The Holy Ghost does; The Spirit of God Leads us into all Truth, and Protect us from all dangers. Was not Joseph Chosen to have the Mind of God, thus enabling him to be knowledgeable by The Will of God for many to be Saved. Only those Saints that has The Mind of God, can have the Vision to be able to know what to do, in order for lives to be Saved. So it is with the Man, who is the head of a Family, with his Wife looking up to him to be the Leader of his Family by

The Will and Favor of God, to protect the Best Kept Secret which is wrapped up in the Woman and Man, to bring forth Inheritance that will Manifest The Greater Glory and Secrets that we that are living now, cannot Accomplish. We have Read The Bible many times, and it Reveals Great things that the People of God will be able to Accomplish, then we look on our capabilities and level of Spirituality and ask the question; how am I going to be able to Accomplish that which is Destined for The Saint of God to Accomplish; but the Truth and the Secret is: We move from Glory to Glory, and from one level of Holiness to another level of Holiness by The Secret of God's Inheritance. While it remain, and it is right now that we are not at the level, if we only lead our Family well, being Men and Leaders of our Family in The Will of God, then God will Do the rest, by Allowing The Greater Glory to be Poured upon our Generation to come, that the Secret which was Hidden in The Power of God, will now be the Manifestation of The Glory of God in the Future.

Just imagine this: The Glory of God started with A Righteous Seed which started with us or our Parents; not because we were worthy of this Honor, but because God Gave us The Spirit to Obey His Commandment; because The Bible Said that it took His Righteousness to make us Righteous, because our righteousness is reckoned to filthy rags. Therefore one level of Glory started with us or our Parents, then another level of Glory is Poured upon our Children which is God's Inheritance / Secret; then as long as the Training is continued from Generation to Generation, we can expect and anticipate that God will Pour upon our third, fourth, fifth and continue to Pour His Glory upon our Generation which is His Inheritance for Him to Receive an Higher Praise and Worship, which results in A Kingdom of Righteousness, which to us now is known as God's Best Kept Secret. So shall a man leave his father and his mother and cling to his wife. The Secrets of God will never be completely realized if The Circle isn't closed. I know many people will not be pleased, because many people or Couples still want and need for their parents to have a strong influence in their now Marriage Relationship, which cannot work and will never work.

We cannot involve outsiders to be a part of the now CLOSED CIRCLE, because we will end up finding ourselves living the lives that our Father and Mother have lived. And in many cases, Mommy and Daddy Relationship did not last, they could not stand the Test that comes with Marriage, if it is that they were Married; and it is even worse if we allow the influence of our Single Parent or Un Married Parents to have a say in our Relationship Manifested by God. And then these are the persons we cling to, in order to obtain advice of how to treat your now Completed Circle, which will not remain Complete, if there is the Influence of someone or different Minds apart from The Mind of God to lead our Circle. Different Minds bring forth different spirits which is Divination, broken down to be Division which is Confusion, and therefore causing our Relationship to have different Attitudes; and different Attitudes is what will break or stop the Best Kept Secret from being realized. One of the main thing to understand, is that God has already Put all the Ingredience inside the Marriage for it to stand every Test that may ever come. One of the main purpose of Marriage is to now depart from one level of Glory of which we are accustomed, to now be born into the new level of Glory that God will now Make to be a Revelation before our very eyes, but the Circle has to be closed.

Marriage is about obtaining the Training that we grew up with, which has a Foundation being of God, then when we have entered into A Marriage Relationship, it is for us now to make our own mistakes in the Circle, and in the very Circle seek to correct those mistake without the influence of outsiders; we have got to remember, that once God is The Foundation, there is nothing He cannot Fix, which may be broken or scarred, because we are the Clay and God is The Creator or every vessel. Inside every Relationship Destined by God, is The Power of The Alpha and Omega, which is to Find Suitable Words, that will be Manifested in our lives to solve every problem.

The Best Kept Secret, in a Nut Shell: "AS LONG AS WE ARE OF THE RIGHTEOUS SEED AND OUR GENERATION IS TRAINED TO FOLLOW THE RIGHTEOUS PATH, THEN PERFECTION WILL

BE OBTAIN, AND OUR CHILDREN CHILDREN'S WILL REAP THE BENEFITS OF PERFECTION".

I Give Honor and Praise to The Mighty God, The King of all kings and The Supreme Ruler of all Ages, Jesus Christ The Only Living God. I hope this Message was Inspiring to all those who have read this Message. I seek to remain A Humble Servant, A Vessel for God to Use; I only ask that you continue to Pray my strength in The Powerful Name Of Jesus Christ. Truly honored, Pastor Lerone Dinnall.

THE BEST KEPT SECRET.

LET US DO IT FOR OUR CHILDREN

Message # 58

Date Started February 17, 2018.
Date Finalized February 17, 2018.

GENESIS CHAPTER 39:7-12. "AND IT CAME TO PASS AFTER THESE THINGS, THAT HIS MASTER'S WIFE CAST HER EYES UPON JOSEPH, AND SHE SAID, LIE WITH ME. BUT HE REFUSED, AND SAID UNTO HIS MASTER'S WIFE, BEHOLD, MY MASTER WOTTETH NOT WHAT IS WITH ME IN THE HOUSE, AND HE HATH COMMITTED ALL THAT HE HATH TO MY HAND; THERE IS NONE GREATER IN THIS HOUSE THAN I; NEITHER HATH HE KEPT BACK ANY THING FROM ME BUT THEE, BECAUSE THOU ART HIS WIFE: HOW THEN CAN I DO THIS GREAT WICKEDNESS, AND SIN AGAINST GOD? AND IT CAME TO PASS, AS SHE SPAKE TO JOSEPH DAY BY DAY, THAT HE HEARKENED NOT UNTO HER, TO LIE BY HER, OR TO BE WITH HER. AND IT CAME TO PASS ABOUT THIS TIME, THAT JOSEPH WENT INTO THE HOUSE TO DO HIS BUSINESS; AND THERE WAS NONE OF THE MEN OF THE

HOUSE THERE WITHIN. AND SHE CAUGHT HIM BY HIS GARMENT, SAYING, LIE WITH ME: AND HE LEFT HIS GARMENT IN HER HAND, AND FLED, AND GOT HIM OUT".

All Honor, Glory to The Most Excellent Father, Jesus Christ The Saviour of Mankind. It is a Privilege that I'm found to be in this Position, yet another time to speak on A Inspiring Topic, that will no doubt, help in The Development of God's Chosen Inheritance. I got this Topic a long time ago, but was just not Inspired till now; having been awaken out of sleep at the time of 1:30am in the morning of February 17, 2018; with A Vision of Threat towards my future Generation Legacy in God. And The Vision is a Great Temptation to be involved with someone who is definitely not my wife, with the promise of that other person that is willing to agree with such an unhealthy relationship, they are making the promise of secrecy, that whatever we have done together will remain a Secret for life, and no one will ever know about it.

FREE WILL; this is where The True Character of A Child of God is Tested; A Servant of God that is Conscious of The Now Active Relationship that they have with CHRIST; that Child of God must now be of The Mindset of which Joseph had, to know that even if this pathway of Temptation crosses their path, of which it will, that Child of God Must now have The Eyes to See and to Foresee that their Relationship that they have Developed with God will never be Compromised for pleasures that will not doubt Destroy The Inheritance of their future Generation, as it was the case of our Forefathers Adam and Eve.

And I'm not even putting my Focused on The Relationship that A Child of God has with their Wife or Husband, but I'm Focusing on The Relationship that A Child God would have Developed, that which we have worked so hard to Established, through years of Fastings and Prayers, Reading and Understanding The Words of God, which would have Manifested in us A Unique Touch from The Heavenly Father; that Relationship that causes many to be at AWE, when it comes on to The Operation of The Holy Ghost in such A Believer's Life. When we consider the High Risk of Losing

God's Special Anointing that Moves Mountains in our lives; will the pleasure of a secret relationship with another person be worth the Decease Infection that will now be Released upon our Future Generation? And I'm not speaking about receiving the Virus of H.I.V. I'm rather speaking and making known to my Readers that, that which we would taken for granted for a few moment of Pleasure; that few moments of pleasure will sometimes spread throughout the Complete Lifetime of our Generation that is to come after us. A Decease that is spread in our D.N.A for All Season and for All Times. Is one day or few moments of sin worth the Sure RISK of Damaging The Legacy of our Future Generation? I don't think so!

The Relationship that we have Developed with God must now force us not to make any MISTAKES, and definitely not to take any RISK; not even to allow such a Thought to be entered in our Minds; because we would have identified that if our Minds Conceive to perform a Act of Sin, then that very thought would have allowed us to Sin in The Eyes of God. St Matthew Chapter 5:27-28 Says:

"YE HAVE HEARD THAT IT WAS SAID BY THEM OF OLD TIME, THOU SHALT NOT COMMIT ADULTERY: BUT I SAY UNTO YOU, THAT WHOSOEVER LOOKETH ON A WOMAN TO LUST AFTER HER HATH COMMITTED ADULTERY WITH HER ALREADY IN HIS HEART".

Let Us Do It For Our Children. The Father of The Universe Realizes that we have Sinned through The Actions of Adam and Eve, and God Made The Choice to Sacrifice Himself to Save us from Eternal Damnation. So it must be The Mindset in us, that we must become Conscious, that whatever we do now, with the life that we are living for Christ, we must have in view that we are making a Daily Sacrifice to Abstain from the Pleasures of this life that everyone else have no problem to perform, because the truth is, those persons are already Marked; Yes, those that have no problem to do what everyone else is doing in the World, they just don't have a Destiny or an Inheritance to Receive from The Father Above. Sacrifice we Must make; Remaining Clean and Untouched for God's Relationship in us we must Become; being Alert at all times of the Threats of others that will seek to Destroy our Inheritance and our Generation's Blessing, we must become Alert to Activate Walls to Protect ourselves and The Future of our Generation.

LET US DO IT FOR OUR CHILDREN.

LET US PRAY TOGETHER. FATHER OF HEAVEN AND EARTH, WE COME BEFORE YOU IN THE ESTABLISHED NAME OF JESUS CHRIST, THE NAME THAT IS GIVEN FOR ACCESS TO TOUCH THE FATHER. LORD WE ASK YOU IN THE NAME OF JESUS CHRIST, THAT YOU WILL FORGIVE US OF OUR SINS; THE SINS OF THE PAST; THE SINS OF THE PRESENT, AND DEFINITELY THE SINS OF THE FUTURE, THOSE SINS THAT OUR CHILDREN, AND OUR CHILDREN'S CHILDREN WOULD HAVE COMMITTED BEFORE YOUR EYES. LORD WE ARE CONSCIOUS OF THE FACT THAT WE MUST BE AND BECOME A FOUNDATION PILLAR FOR OUR GENERATION TO COME, THEREFORE FATHER, WE STAND IN THE GAP, AND WE ASK YOU FATHER IN THE NAME OF JESUS CHRIST, THAT YOU WILL HELP US TO STAND UP FOR OUR GENERATION, HELP US TO DO THE ACCEPTABLE THINGS IN YOUR EYES, EVEN IF THOSE THINGS IS GOING TO CAUSE US TO BE IN PRISON; LORD HELP US TO ALWAYS HAVE IN VIEW THE DESTINY OF OUR GENERATION. LORD WE KNOW THAT WE CANNOT DO IT WITHOUT YOU, THEREFORE FATHER WE ASK IN THE NAME OF JESUS CHRIST, THAT YOUR SPIRIT WILL MOVE WITHIN OUR LIVES, WE ASK THAT YOUR SPIRIT WILL MOVE UPON OUR PATH THAT WE SHOULD TAKE, WE ASK THAT YOUR SPIRIT WILL MOVE IN EVERY DECISION THAT WE WILL MAKE, BECAUSE WE HAVE ALREADY IDENTIFY THAT IF YOUR SPIRIT IS ABSENT FROM THAT WHICH WE DO, THEN WE KNOW THAT WE ARE GOING TO FAIL, WE MUST FAIL, AND OUR CHILDREN WILL FAIL BECAUSE THERE IS NO SPIRIT OF GOD TO DIRECT OUR PATHWAY. FATHER OF HEAVEN AND EARTH, WE ASK THAT YOU WILL BREATH UPON US, AS WE COMMIT ALL OUR LIVES AND THE LIVES OF OUR CHILDREN IN YOUR HANDS. FATHER WE ASK IN THE NAME OF JESUS CHRIST THAT YOU WILL GRANT UNTO US THAT ARE PARENTS A RESPONSIBLE SPIRIT, THAT WE WILL NOT FAIL YOUR WILL FOR OUR LIVES AND THE

LIVES OF OUR CHILDREN TO COME. HELP US TO BECOME EXAMPLES FOR YOU IN A DYING WORLD; HELP US TO BECOME THE PARENTS THAT WILL SAYS NO TO TEMPTATION; HELP US TO TRAIN OUR CHILDREN IN THE RIGHT PATHWAY THAT WILL PLEASE GOD; HELP US TO NOT COMPROMISE WITH YOUR LAWS FOR OUR LIVES; HELP US TO STAND FATHER, HELP US; BECAUSE WE CAN DO NOTHING WITHOUT YOU. THIS IS OUR REQUEST OUR FATHER IN THE NAME OF JESUS CHRIST LET YOUR WILL BE DONE IN OUR LIVES HAS IT IS THAT YOUR WILL IS ESTABLISHED IN HEAVEN ABOVE, AMEN, AMEN AND AMEN.

We can say that this Message is for The Parents that are SERIOUS about their Generation's Inheritance. We can do it for our Children; We MUST Stand up for our Children; in The Mighty Name of Jesus Christ We will Stand up for our Children. God will Grant us The Strength to become The Generation that will Do what is Required for us to DO in The Name of Jesus Christ.

From The Ministry of The Church of Jesus Christ Fellowship Savannah Cross Ltd. This Ministry will Continue to Pray for Marriages and Couples in God, and while this Church continue to Pray for Marriages and Couples in God, I ask that you do likewise and offer A Prayer for the Continual Success and Establishment of this Ministry, that we may Continue to Touch lives through The Help of God Almighty. Pastor Lerone Dinnall.

STAND UP FOR YOUR GENERATION!

GENERATION FOCUSED

Message # 90   Date Started February 6, 2018
                                Date Finalized February 9, 2018.

GENESIS CHAPTER 21:9-14. "AND SARAH SAW THE SON OF
HAGAR THE EGYPTIAN, WHICH SHE HAD BORN UNTO ABRAHAM,
MOCKING. WHEREFORE SHE SAID UNTO ABRAHAM, CAST OUT
THIS BONDWOMAN AND HER SON: FOR THE SON OF THIS
BONDWOMAN SHALL NOT BE HEIR WITH MY SON, EVEN WITH
ISAAC. AND THE THING WAS VERY GRIEVOUS IN ABRAHAM'S
SIGHT BECAUSE OF HIS SON. AND GOD SAID UNTO ABRAHAM,
LET IT NOT BE GRIEVOUS IN THY SIGHT BECAUSE OF THE LAD,
AND BECAUSE OF THY BONDWOMAN; IN ALL THAT SARAH HATH
SAID UNTO THEE, HEARKEN UNTO HER VOICE; FOR IN ISAAC
SHALL THY SEED BE CALLED. AND ALSO OF THE SON OF THE
BONDWOMAN WILL I MAKE A NATION, BECAUSE HE IS THY
SEED. AND ABRAHAM ROSE UP EARLY IN THE MORNING, AND
TOOK BREAD, AND A BOTTLE OF WATER, AND GAVE IT UNTO
HAGAR, PUTTING IT ON HER SHOULDER, AND THE CHILD, AND

SENT HER AWAY: AND SHE DEPARTED, AND WANDERED IN THE WILDERNESS OF BEERSHEBA".

To God be All The Glory, Honor and Praise; happy am I to be in this Position, yet another time to speak on a Topic, that will no doubt Inspire those who will read this Message. It is Staggering to see and to come to the realization that there is a lot of people, Couples and especially Saints that are not Knowledgeable nor do they have the Understanding to have the Discerning to behold that there must be everything done in one's power, to make sure that we that are Parents make Decisions that will Positively affect our Future Generations. There is found many that are Father's and Mother's to their Children that are just not walking or operating in the capacity of which the Title of Parenthood suggest. There is found many Parents that are just living their lives for themselves; not considering that there is going to be a tomorrow for the Child that comes from their lineage. For many Parents, it is sad to say, but many Parents are Selfish; lack of Wisdom; lack Knowledge; lack of Understanding; which spells that there is definitely a Lack of God's Presence to Lead that Family.

The Bible Said in The Book of Psalms 127:1. "EXCEPT THE LORD BUILD THE HOUSE, THEY LABOUR IN VAIN THAT BUILD IT: EXCEPT THE LORD KEEP THE CITY, THE WATCHMAN WAKETH BUT IN VAIN".

Even though it is sad to discover that there is a lot of Unwise Parents; The Word of God Demonstrate to us that unless a man chooses to build upon The Sure Foundation, then that man will find himself building on Sinking Sand, not only for himself, but also for his entire Generation to come. There is always a Choice, there is always FREEWILL present for every person that is to walk the road of life, weather Saved or not Saved.

I must commend those Parents that are True to the Responsibility that they hold, Parents that make sure that they have crossed all the T's and dot all the I's. It demonstrates that we are FOCUSED AND SOLID AS A ROCK for ourselves and our Generation to come.

The passage of Scripture describe Sarah the Mother of Isaac, making a Decision, that for many that are living now, under the

Influence and Teaching of the World, would consider that which she did was Evil and Cruel. Even in the eyes of Abraham when he first received the word from his wife, it seemed to be painful. If it was not for The Intervention of God The Almighty that was Leading Abraham's Life, maybe this Opinion of his wife would be a decision that would not have been carried out. It is important to understand has Parents that we need God has our Guide; therefore whatever Decisions that we may face in life, as long as God Gives The Approval, we will not Worry, Wonder, Ponder or be Afraid because we would have Acknowledge that God is in it.

Let us look at The Power of The Word of God. Abraham received the same word from two different personnel; the word from his wife troubled his Heart, gave an Headache to his Mind, and also Frustrated his Soul to Choose. The thought must have also erupted in Abraham to ask himself: "WHAT KIND OF HEART DOES MY WIFE TRULY POSSESS, THAT SHE IS ABLE TO THINK OF SOMETHING LIKE THIS, BECAUSE ISHMAEL WAS IN FACT HIS SON". What a Difference The Word of God Makes; the same word was repeated to Abraham from God, and instead of having a sleepless night, The Bible Said that Abraham rose up early in the morning to Execute that which was now Confirmed by The Mouth of God. Hard Decision, but as long as God is in the Decision making, it simply means that God has already made a way out of no way.

But let us have a look at the wisdom of Sarah: reading this passage of Scripture makes me realize that in Parenthood, one partner will not be able to see everything, make a Note of that Revelation. Nor is it wise for one member of the Family Circle to make all the Decisions, thus one member of the Circle who is the person responsible for making the Decisions, should always Position Himself to Listen and then to Consult God for Directions. It is observed in The Scripture that Sarah could not make the Decision herself, therefore she had to consult her Husband with her concerns. Look at this wisdom; even though Sarah knew what needed to be done, because it was already confirmed within her spirit; it is important to Understand that Sarah knew her Position in the Relationship.

The Man of God Bishop Austin Whitfield would often repeat these words:

"IT'S NOT WHAT IS DONE, BUT RATHER HOW IT WAS DONE".

Bishop Whitfield was making reference to The Saints while Teaching to make us Understand that nothing is wrong with what a person has Discern to fulfill, but rather Lamented that there are Procedures to follow in order to fulfill that which needs to be done, in that he Expressed to the Ministers and Missionaries that they must first consult their Leader before making Decisions.

Could you just imagine Sarah, receiving the Revelation of what needs to be done, and she went ahead and did not consult her Husband of what she had decided to do. Again realize, she saw what needed to be done, but she also knew her place in the Marriage Relationship between herself and Abraham. It is important to Understand our Destiny and the Destiny of our Children, because if we don't understand our Destiny, then we will accept anything that comes our way. Sarah saw, that what Ishmael was doing and Patterning himself to now rule over Isaac, because he was older than Isacc, this Action in the view of Sarah, if it was to continue would be in complete Contradiction of what The DESTINY of Isaac was; Sarah also discovered that hard Decisions had to be made, because she had The Eyes to Discern that as long as Ishmael was around, there was no way Isaac would become and obtained The Promised Destiny that God Has Spoken.

There are always Obstacles in the pathway of our Destiny, that's the main reason why The Lord Ask us to Search The Scriptures for in them ye think ye have Eternal life. The Revelation of life's Decisions or Crossroads can only be achieved if a Saint of God have Birth The Fruit of Responsibility to Protect our Destiny. I was speaking to someone the other day, and I said to that person that everything that God Has Given to His People for a Gift, it requires for that person to now have the Discipline to know that it is going to require now a lot of HARD WORK to Maintain and to Keep that Gift. There are many that believe that once we've Received something from God, there will be no Maintenance necessary for us to keep that Gift. Children are

Gifts from God, there are many Parents that can testify to the fact that they have seen a lot of Couples that desires to have a child, and no matter what they do, they just cannot have a child; then on the other hand, it is found a Couple, that does not necessarily have all the condition that is required to facilitate a Child; that's the Couple The Lord Chooses to Smile on, therefore Allowing that Couple to bring forth a seed for God's Inheritance and also for the continuation of that Couples Generation. A Marriage Partner is a Gift that only God can Give, meaning that it must be in the full Influence of God that a person or Saint makes the Decision to enter into a Marriage Covenant with another Person. I 've been Instructing the Future Generation of The Church to ensure that those who they would desire to Married; they must make certain that those persons Resembles the Full Manifestation of God; because it is a Fact, you are going to Vow your Entire life over to the will and desire of that same person; therefore be WARNED!

It is important for Couples to understand that if God Brings us to The Blessing / Gift, there is no doubt, that God has already made Provisions in His Plans exactly how that Gift or Blessing will be Sustained. Trust for God and His Word is the Key; I don't see the way, but I know that God has already Made The Way for myself and for all The Gifts that he has Given unto His People. A Word of Revelation for Couples that desires to have children and have not received any as yet; and also for those Couples that have children and is considering if they should have more children. Every Couple before God's Eye is considered to be a Tree; especially those who God has Joined together; because it's not everyone God has joined together, some of us joined ourselves together. Getting back to what I was saying: Couples are Productive Tree before God's Eye and for His Specific Will be Done; when it is that this Tree has been watered and it so Pleases God, that this Tree should bring forth Fruit; The Lord Will now Allow for this Tree to spring forth a New Branch which was never there before, just to facilitate the New Addition to the family of that Tree.

David said in The Book of Psalms 37:25.

"I HAVE BEEN YOUNG, AND NOW AM OLD; YET HAVE I NOT SEEN THE RIGHTEOUS FORSAKEN, NOR HIS SEED BEGGING BREAD".

These are not only the Confirmation of David's Knowledge, but it is also THE COVENANT PROMISE OF GOD ALMIGHTY. The Key however is to Learn how to Trust God for The Direction of our Family.

The most important Mission in life for Couples is definitely not our Jobs, because our jobs will pass, and we may even lose our Jobs; it's definitely not our Money, because it will fly away; not the Car or the House it will get old one day; it's not even ourselves or our Position in life or Possessions. The most important Mission for our lives is to Be and to Remain FOCUSED ON OUR GENERATION, JUST LIKE SARAH. The Gift to See and to Foresee what is to come in the Future is A Gift that only God can Give. And this is The Gift that Sarah was Blessed to have. On the other hand, we cannot be unwise like our Forefathers, meaning Adam and Eve. They made Decisions based upon their own Selfish Desires and the ENVY of God's Authority; they did not have The Gift to See and to Foresee, meaning Discern, to come to the Understanding to be Knowledgeable that whatever Decisions they made would have Ultimately Paved the Pathway for their Generations to Follow. So is it laid on us as Couples, to make sure that we Learn from the Mistakes of the Past, and seek to help create a future with the Destiny that God has Approved.

In order for a Couple that is Serving God to become Generation Focused, that Couple has to be Born in The Spirit of God, to become of the Attitude that they will not allow any unwanted seed of DESTINY DESTROYER to be Sown in the life of their Present life, and also in the life of their Future Generation. The Couple that God has Chosen for Destiny has to become Aware of their own Destiny in God and that of their own Generation, to therefore now become of the Attitude that they are STERN in every Decision making, which will in fact create the Future for their own Generation. I don't mean to be repeating myself, but I need those who are Serious about their Generation to be Born in the Understanding that they must do everything that is Possible to Protect and to Guide their Generation, even if it means that others is going to be Upset with your Decisions. Born Again Couples have got to Set themselves to become Flexible to Change, meaning at any or every given time the Atmosphere and the Environment changes to a negative, that will speak a different pathway to your Destiny and the Destiny of your Children, that Couple that is being Lead by The Spirit of God will now be Given The Approval of The Eyes to Discern that their must now be a Change in direction of the Pathway of their own Family. Serious Times Couples of God, these are Serious Times. The Foolish will be Destroyed and The Wise in Heart and Mind are the ones that will Survive to Protect their Generation and Secure The Divine Destiny. If we could recall the Story and the Pathway of Baby Jesus; this was a life and a journey that had a lot of Travelling; a lot of Sudden changes from town to town, just to preserve The Coming Messiah's Destiny from the hands of those who were assigned to kill him. And this was in Fact The Son of The Living God! How much those of us who are offspring's of this same Jesus Christ.

The God Lead Couple will now have to move according to The Wave of The Spirit of God, which means that there will be Constant Decisions that are necessary to be made for Change. The Couple that is being Lead by The Spirit of God will in fact at time be Called to Change their Company, because if the Company does not Reflect The Destined Inheritance of God, then that Company will stop those who are Destined for The Inheritance of God. Some Companies, no matter how hard a person tries to change those persons to The Will of God, it will turn around that those person will change you and your Generation from Divine Destiny; those persons or company does not have The Seed of Growth in them to Aspire A Child of God to Grow. There are some Couples that are Naive towards their own Divine Destiny, and God Has not Given us The Spirit to become Simple, but Rather, The Lord Has Given us The Spirit of His Intelligence, therefore Wise Christian we must Become. The Couples that is being Lead by The Spirit of God will Discern that they will have to Change their Surroundings; being Children of Destiny, we have to become

Fast to Understand the spirits that are Governing the Environment and the Atmosphere that ourselves and our Children is being allowed to breath in; because if there is not the Eyes to Discover the spirits of the Environment and Atmosphere, we will be Trapped in that very Atmosphere and Environment that Dictates what the Destiny of our lives and the lives of our Generation will Become.

A Physical man cannot tell the Difference of an Environment or Atmosphere; it take a Spiritual Man to identify an Atmosphere of which when it is now identified, that Spiritual Man makes certain that The Spirit's full Attention is now Activated to Allow him to Discern the Threats of that same Environment; therefore preventing the Conformation or Adaptation of that Environment to now Strangle the life of The Fresh Anointing that does Exist in that Spiritual Man. This Revelation is for those who are Born in the Understanding of A New Level of Anointing; therefore ordinary Christians will not identify what The Spirit of God is Revealing. Because if a Saint have not yet Graduated to A New Level of Anointing, whatsoever is spoken of concerning The New Level Anointing will in fact be a Mystery to those who have not yet Tasted that The New Level Anointing does Exist.

Just have a look at this for a minute; Abraham before God Called him to Separate Himself from his own Country and Kindred; this same Abraham was not poor, he was not the worse among his brethren; but The Spirit of God gave Abraham a Charge, Saying:

"GET THEE OUT OF THY COUNTRY, AND FROM THY KINDRED, AND FROM THY FATHER'S HOUSE, UNTO A LAND THAT I WILL SHEW THEE: AND I WILL MAKE OF THEE A GREAT NATION, AND I WILL BLESS THEE, AND MAKE THY NAME GREAT; AND THOU SHALT BE A BLESSING: AND I WILL BLESS THEM THAT BLESS THEE, AND CURSE HIM THAT CURSETH THEE: AND IN THEE SHALL ALL FAMILIES OF THE EARTH BE BLESSED". Genesis Chapter 12:1-3.

In order for God to Take His People and Couples of The Church to New Level of Anointing, there must be SEPARATION from the Environment that they have now Accustomed themselves to be a part of. The Lord is not Calling us to Hate People, but rather to become Different, to Change from a lifestyle of Simple to be Born in a lifestyle that we have Become Wise to the Touch, that we Identify that the Most Important Mission of Life is to do all that is necessary to make certain that we Protect The Destiny of our own Generation. God Needed to Bless Abraham but He Could Not Bless him in his Current Environment and Beliefs. Divine Blessings can never be Mixed with Physical Attractions and lifestyle of Spiritual Barrenness.

I believe that this Message is Geared specifically for Saints or Sons of God, because it's only Saints and Sons of God that can in Fact Claim that they have an Inheritance to Possess.

In Closing, I will ask this Question: What is Preventing us from making a change from Spiritual Barrenness of our own Generation's Destiny to Spiritual Production of our same Generation's Destiny? That's a question that only the man in the Mirror can answer!

LET US PRAY; FATHER OF HEAVEN AND EARTH, I CALL UPON YOU THROUGH THE ONLY ACCESS OF THE NAME OF JESUS CHRIST, THE ONLY SAVING NAME AND ACCESS DOOR TO THE FATHER. I ASK FATHER, THAT YOU WILL FORGIVE YOUR PEOPLE OF OUR SINS; SINS OF THE PAST, SINS OF THE PRESENT, AND ESPECIALLY THOSE SINS OF THE FUTURE THAT OUR CHILDREN AND OUR CHILDREN'S CHILDREN WOULD HAVE COMMITTED BEFORE YOUR EYES. FATHER, WE ARE AS CHILDREN IN YOUR EYES, WE KNOW NOT HOW TO GO OUT OR TO COME IN, UNLESS YOUR SPIRIT LEADS US IN THE PATHWAY THAT WE SHOULD TAKE. FATHER, I REMIND YOU OF YOUR WORDS, IN THAT YOU SAID THAT CHILDREN ARE AN HERITAGE OF THE LORD AND THE FRUIT OF THE WOMB IS YOUR REWARD. FATHER, I CALL UPON YOU IN THE NAME OF JESUS CHRIST, THAT YOU WILL RELEASE YOUR SPIRIT OF INTELLIGENCE UPON THE LIVES OF YOUR CHOSEN PEOPLE, THAT WE WILL BE BORN IN THE UNDERSTANDING TO KNOW EXACTLY WHAT IT IS THAT WE NEED TO DO, IN ORDER FOR US TO MAKE WISE DECISIONS THAT WILL PAVE THE PATHWAY FOR THE GENERATION THAT IS TO COME. THIS WISDOM FATHER OF HEAVEN CAN ONLY COME FROM

YOU. HELP US FATHER, HAS YOU HELPED THE CHILDREN OF ISRAEL TO BECOME STRONG BEFORE THEIR ENEMIES. HELP US TO UNDERSTAND THAT WE CANNOT MIX OUR GENERATION WITH THE SEED OF THE HEATHEN GENERATION THAT DOES NOT BELIEVE IN YOU. FATHER HELP US TO BECOME RIGID AND STERN TO MAKE CERTAIN THAT WE DO EVERYTHING THAT IS IN OUR POWER TO DO, TO MAKE CERTAIN AT ALL COST THAT WE PROTECT THE FUTURE OF OUR GENERATION. HELP US TO BE OBEDIENT CHILDREN, THAT WE WILL WALK IN YOUR PRECEPTS, LAWS AND COMMANDMENTS; FATHER WE PRAY IN THE NAME OF JESUS CHRIST THAT YOU WILL HELP; OUR FATHER MUST HELP; HEAVENLY FATHER WILL ALWAYS HELP, GUIDE AND PROTECT HIS CHOSEN INHERITANCE, BECAUSE THE RIGHTEOUS MUST INHERIT THE EARTH ACCORDING TO THE WORDS OF THE LORD. THESE REQUEST WE PUT BEFORE YOU FATHER IN THE NAME OF JESUS CHRIST; AND WE ALL SAY AMEN, AMEN AND AMEN.

To God be all The Glory, Honor and Praise; in The Mighty Saving Name of Jesus Christ. From The Ministry of The Church of Jesus Christ Fellowship Savannah Cross Ltd. Stay Firm in God and God will Stay FIRM for you and your Generation. Pastor Lerone Dinnall.

GENERATION FOCUSED. ARE YOU FOCUSED FOR YOUR GENERATION?

FROM UGLY TO PRETTY

Message # 78   Date Started August 24, 2017
                                                    Date Finalized August 24, 2017.

FOR THOSE WHO ARE Still wondering if Christianity is the Right Choice.
FATHER OF HEAVEN, IN THE NAME OF JESUS CHRIST OF
NAZARETH, THE LAMB OF GOD, THROUGH WHICH ALL ACCESS
IS GRANTED FOR ALL THOSE WHO BELIEVE IN YOUR NAME. I
APPROACH MY LORD KNOWING THAT THOU ART THE GOD OF
ABRAHAM, THE GOD OF ISACC AND THE GOD OF ALL ISRAEL;
THEREFORE THERE IS NOTHING THAT THOU CANNOT DO. I PRAY
AT THIS TIME FOR THE MINDS OF THOSE WHO ARE CALLED BY
YOU TO FULFILL THEIR PURPOSE IN YOU, KNOWING THAT THE
ENEMY WILL NOT REST UNLESS HE CAUSES YOUR PEOPLE TO
FALL BY THE INFLUENCES OF THE WORLD. LORD I PRAY THAT
THOU O LORD WILL GRANT UNTO YOUR PEOPLE A STRONG
WILL, THAT IN SPITE AND DESPITE OF THE CHALLENGES THAT
WE FACE, WE WILL BE ABLE BY THE POWER OF YOUR BLOOD
TO OVERCOME. LORD, LET YOUR PEOPLE WHICH ARE CALLED
BY YOUR NAME RECOGNIZE THAT THIS LIFE IS ONLY OUR TEST;

LET US RECOGNIZE WHO WE WERE BEFORE WE KNEW YOU, HELP US TO ROLL BACK THE CURTAINS OF PAST MEMORIES, SHOW US WHERE YOU'VE BROUGHT US FROM AND WHAT WE COULD HAVE BECOME; AND ALSO HELP US TO UNDERSTAND WHO WE ARE NOW, AND OUR DESTINY IN YOU, WHICH CAN ONLY BE REALIZED IF ONLY WE HAVE OBTAINED THE WILL AND MINDSET TO CONTINUE WITH THE LIVING GOD. LORD, THOU KNOWETH THE VERY END FROM THE BEGINNING OF TIME, THOU ART KNOWLEDGEABLE CONCERNING THOSE WHO ARE THE TITHES OF SAINTS; GIVE O LORD YOUR PEOPLE A PERFECT UNDERSTANDING, TO STAND UP FOR HOLINESS, THAT WE WILL BE ABLE TO REPRESENT THE LIKENESS OF WHO YOU ARE, THAT WE CAN REMAIN BEING THE TITHES OF SAINTS. LORD THOU ART ALPHA AND OMEGA, THE BEGINNING AND THE ENDING, THE FIRST AND THE LAST, THE SOLID ROCK ON WHICH WE STAND. I PRAY ONLY IN THE NAME OF JESUS CHRIST THAT THOU O GOD WILL RELEASE AN ANOINTING UPON YOUR CHOSEN PEOPLE, THAT WE WILL HAVE THE STRENGTH TO STAND UP FOR GOD; HELP US TO STAND O LORD, HELP US TO STAND IN THE NAME OF JESUS CHRIST HELP US TO STAND, AMEN.

Greetings in The Mighty Name of Jesus Christ our Saviour and Soon Coming King. Again it is a Wonderful opportunity to be able to write Messages like this for God's Chosen People, to be able to be an Instrument to help Strengthen the Belief of God's People. We are living in a World that every turn we make, there is something there to influence the life of a Child of God, not to believe in the Power of The Almighty God; therefore to have Inspired Message like this, even for myself and personal Family and also Church Family, is found to be a Breath of Fresh Air from the Father Above. A Reminder that God is Still Speaking Words of Encouragement to the Lives of His People.

We have here a Topic that says, From Ugly to Pretty; the first and main thing we want to have a look on is the word Ugly. Now according to the Webster's Dictionary, the word Ugly means: Very unattractive or displeasing in appearance. Disagreeable; Objectionable. And I like the meaning that is next. Morally Revolting. The word Revolting means that such a person is Disgusting; Repulsive or Rebellious. Of which when we add the word Morally to that word Revolting, it means that to this life, this person is not accepted, they are Rejected; is found to be in a condition, that the only use now is for us to be thrown away. I need my Readers to consider very careful the meaning of this word the next time the devil and his demons entice us to commit a Sin, because if we have yielded to the Attractions and Temptations of the Devil, then we are opening back the door that leads to us becoming who we were before God Found us. Here is something we never even consider; when we were in this type of Deplorable condition, those who are Enticing us to commit Sin now, did they even know us, much less to speak to us. And because has the Bible said, that My People are destroyed for a Lack of Knowledge. We now find ourselves in the same capacity to be destroyed of the devil because we have not yet realized that the devil is all mouth and no action, his main job is to deceive, and he has a Eternity perfecting his craft, therefore he has the Master's Certificate, Diploma and PHD of knowing how to deceive God's People. Bishop Austin Whitfield said the Devil has seven different pen, to write seven different challenges for the life of God's People to face at different times in their lives.

I don't know about you, but coming to God and Accepting God is the Best decision I've ever made. Coming from a life when I was a Child, I knew what it felt like to be Ugly, with every turn I make, the statement was the same that I even started to believe what was now being said. If it was not for God that Saw it best to Speak to a Child like me, which saw people singing the song over my life, that I'm a Nobody and is destined to be a Nobody. The Voice of God Spoke when I was just a little Child, and Said:

"I'M GOING TO MAKE A PERSON WHO IS A NOBODY INTO A SOMEBODY". The song writer said: "IF IT HAD NOT BEEN, FOR THE LORD ON MY SIDE, TELL ME WHERE WOULD I BE, WHERE WOULD I BE"? Nowhere, I would still be in a Position to be considered a Nobody.

The Book of Isaiah Chapter 6:5. Described Isaiah has being truly

Humbled and Unworthy of the Call that God had bestowed upon his life.

"THEN SAID I, WOE IS ME! FOR I AM UNDONE; BECAUSE I AM OF UNCLEAN LIPS, AND I DWELL IN THE MIDST OF A PEOPLE OF UNCLEAN LIPS: FOR MINE EYES HAVE SEEN THE KING, THE LORD OF HOST".

How many of us truly recognize what God has taken us from; what God has Separated us from? If we don't know what we were, then we can never appreciate what God has now made us to become. We have to Understand the Past life, to be able to Treat the New Life as Precious Gold. So Precious that we cannot afford to make our foot, not even to slip for a Second, because we would have remembered that we were a Nobody; Dirt; Filth, Unclean, Unworthy and Far away from God's Mercy. I don't know if any of my Readers had a good life before they met God; I know I didn't. Therefore with every Breath, with every Step, every Speech, every Imagination of thoughts of the Mind, I need to make sure that I Honour The Name of Jesus Christ, The Only Living God. While there is in the Mind of others that there is always a second chance; in my Mind, there is No Second Chance, there is only One Opportunity to make my Calling an Election Sure. What say You?

From Ugly to Pretty, here is the Big Question:

"WHICH OF THE TWO ARE YOU"?

To The Lord Jesus Christ be all The Glory, Honour and Praise. I hope this Message has been an Inspiration to your Christian Walk, continue to Pray for this Ministry. Pastor Lerone Dinnall.

FROM UGLY TO PRETTY...

THE SEVEN DISCIPLINES TO OBSERVE; THE SECRETS OF HOW TO REMAIN BLESSED

Message # 31   **Date Started October 10, 2016**
Date Finalized October 31, 2016.

I LOVE GOD TOO much to fail Him now. I Greet all My Fathers Children in The Wonderful Matchless Name of Jesus Christ, our Soon Coming King. Honored am I, and also privileged to be in a Position that God can Speak through me, that others can be Blessed. You may wonder why I said this; this is the reason: I went to the Super Market today October 10th, 2016; and I met someone that I gave a Message, about two months ago; the person came to me, and said of a truth I knew I was going to see you today; I asked why; the person said that when I gave the Message to him, he place it one side, and never had a look on it, until two days before now, being the 8th of October 2016. The person went on to say that he and his wife took the Message and began reading; the person told me that the Message was speaking directly to him and his wife, in that they could not put the Message down, until they have fully read all the information, and all the information was about ten (10) sheets; this they did, and also confess that they were only prepared to read one (1) page for that night. The person was also asking me permission to use the Message as an Exaltation to be done in his Church. For this I felt very pleased, to know that God is receiving His Glory from what He Asked me to Do. Someone, if it is at least one person is being helped by these Messages. With that being said, let us now turn our attention to the Message at hand. Let us seek to help one more Soul to have a Closer grip on their Salvation. The Message says: "THE SEVEN DISCIPLINES TO OBSERVE; THE SECRETS OF HOW TO REMAIN BEING BLESSED". Now you may not know, but the Secrets to Eternal Life can only be found in The Word of God; the Secrets to True Peace rest in The MIND of GOD; the Secrets for every individual's Blessings is found in The Spirit of GOD.

I looked around, and I observe that this World Teaches its occupants that the only way to be happy; to have joy; to have peace; is to follow with all their Heart, Mind and Soul, that which the World needs them to follow after. I've also observed that many of us; even in The Church, are blinded by the illusions of the World, that we as Servants of God, also become blinded by the disguise that the World has unfolded before our eyes; and yes this is sad; but it is not the end; because while we still have breath and there is still the evidence of The Word of God in us, there remains HOPE; we can still make it; we can still be an Overcomer; the scales can still be removed from our eyes, to allow us to see what is the True Love that God has for us all. Everyone needs to be Blessed, it's only a Fool alone would reject Blessing; especially the Blessings that comes from God with A Divine Purpose and not a Permitted purpose. But there still remain one important FACT; which is:

"RECEIVING THE BLESSING IS ONE LEVEL; BUT HAVING THE DISCIPLINE TO KEEP THE BLESSING GOES WAY ABOVE THE LEVEL OF WHAT YOU RECEIVED".

Keeping the Blessing takes a lot of Discipline and Hard Work.

Being A Child of God, I don't want to run this race in vain; but to ensure that it was a productive race. It is amazing to see that The Lord Uses the number Seven in most of His Revelations, as it is now being used again; Seven is considered to be God's Perfect Number. Reading The Bible carefully, no one can doubt the Fact that God has Destined for His People a life of Blessing; but there is also the Fact, that although God has Destined Blessings for His People, the enemy still tries his best to destroy or to delay The Blessing that is Divinely placed for The Righteous Seed. And this is where this Message comes in; to be a Guideline for God's People to know what is important, that each man having received his Blessing, will be able to put on the necessary protection that is needed in order to keep the Blessings that God have Bestowed upon our lives. God's Intentions for His People are only Good; with Desiring to Produce a Good Work, that will last throughout all Generations; The Lord Speaking to Himself in though said:

"LET US MAKE MAN IN OUR OWN IMAGE, AFTER OUR LIKENESS". Genesis 1:26.

This event started the beginning of the Blessings that God had in store for His People; which was later stolen by the enemy using the spirit of Envy to sway the Mind of Eve and then Adam to Disobey that which God Commanded them not to DO. If we should read verse 31 of Genesis Chapter 1. It will no doubt explain that all that God has made was considered to be Very Good in His Eyes. How many stories in The Bible do you Recognize, that God's People receive their Blessings, but was just not able to hold on to The Blessings that God Has Imparted upon His People; How many time?

The Book of Judges is filled with the experiences of God's People; Their rise through Righteousness, and then their destructive fall through Disobedience; and the cycle goes on, and on and on, throughout the whole Bible; throughout all Generations. And one thing that I've discovered that keeps allowing this to happen, is the Fact, that God's People are not Discipline enough to follow the Guidelines of that which God Command them to Follow; and also while you find yourself following the Guide Lines / Statues of God, to make sure that you Teach the Generation to come; especially your Children and those that are of your household. The Bible Said:

"MY PEOPLE ARE DESTROYED FOR A LACK OF KNOWLEDGE". Hosea 4:6.

We can actually judge ourselves, by asking ourselves this Question: "When we Failed, was it because we were well knowledgeable of God's Commandments, or was it because we were not aware of what The Words of God asked us to Maintained"? I know it's the latter, you should too. Let us have a look on The Seven Disciplines / Secrets, of how to remain being Blessed. This Topic is not like other Messages that we stick to one Topic, the Message however has Seven Disciplines that we are going to look into, and discover the Truth of how to remain being Blessed. We must be well aware by now, that the Mind of a man, controls the whole body of that man; therefore the first Discipline is:

TO FREE / CLEANSE OUR MIND FROM INIQUITY # 1. Reason, the first place in the life of a man, in the life of a Child of God that can be corrupted is the Mind; and once the Mind of a Child of God is changed from being focused on God; then the whole direction of that person is now changed from light to darkness; because the corrupt Mind now feeds the corrupt information to the heart that will now become corrupt; the heart then distribute all the corrupt information of the Mind to the members of the body; thus causing the whole body to now become corrupt, but it starts with the Mind. What do you think happened to Adam and Eve; the enemy found a way to plant a Seed of Envy in the Mind of God Created Beings; which then open the door to their own destruction. 1 Peter 1:13. Spoke to us as Saints, advising us that we should gird up the loins of our Mind, to be Sober, and hope to the end for the Grace that it to be brought unto you at the Revelation of Jesus Christ. Becoming Children of God we have to see it as our main duty to make sure that we guard the part of our lives that is Spiritual; because the Spiritual brings forth the manifestation to everything that is Physical; therefore if you need to observe Physical breakthrough, you have to make sure that there is a Spiritual Breakthrough. If the Mind is sick and filled with Iniquity, then the whole body will never be able to fulfill the Requirement of GOD, nor will you be in the position to ask God for anything, that will demand, that God will Answer your request. The Bible said:

"IF YE ABIDE IN ME, AND MY WORDS ABIDE IN YOU, YE SHALL ASK WHAT YE WILL, AND IT SHALL BE DONE UNTO YOU". St John 15:7.

Learn this, Lucifer only conceived in his Mind that he was going to build his kingdom above The Most High God; only that thought of Envy conceived by the devil, was sufficient enough, to remove him from Heaven and erase his place forever in The Kingdom of God. Did not The Lord said that:

"THOU SHALT NOT COMMIT ADULTERY: BUT I SAY UNTO YOU, THAT WHOSOEVER LOOKETH ON A WOMAN TO LUST AFTER HER HATH COMMITTED ADULTERY WITH HER ALREADY IN HIS HEART". St Matthew 5:27&28.

The Mind conceives; leads to the heart desiring to do; without action, in The Eyes of God, we have sin. This World Teaches us that if the action is not done; then the desire is not carried out. The Word of God Teaches us, that if you but just for a minute LUST, which is a desire to have; then that desire will cause us to sin, even though no action was done. The number one weapon that the enemy seeks to use on God's People, is to dangle a Carrot before our eyes, to see if we would desire to lust after that Carrot; the Carrot can be a Car, a House, a Wife, a Husband, a Job or some other opportunity. Remember that Lust is a desire to have; therefore let us be careful of what we desire to have; it will lead to sin, if it is outside of The Will of GOD. All the other Disciplines fall under the Discipline of the Mind, to guard against Iniquity. This means that, if the Discipline of the Mind is not secure to cleanse itself of Iniquity; then the other six Disciplines won't be able to be maintained; they cannot stand because The Spiritual part of a man is now affected, thus no Fruits can bear.

DISCIPLINE # 2. **IS OBEDIENCE,** I can just hear a lot of people saying No! Because they don't think the order is correct; and I can understand why you would say that; because I grow up along with my fellow Readers, being Taught in Sunday School that Disobedience is the Only Sin; of which this is correct, but let us take a closer look to seek to understand; why would a Child of God even have the appetite in the first place, to even want to Obey that which God Commanded! The True answer is the MIND, the Spiritual part of that man is now in agreement with The Word of GOD; therefore if the Mind is FOCUSED on God, then it is much easier for that Child of GOD to be Obedient; that was the reason why the Serpent attacked the Mind of Eve, and after she was fully convinced, meaning the seed of the Serpent was sown; she then sowed that very same seed of ENVY to her Husband, which allowed them to fall out of Fellowship with God. Therefore The Lord Revealed to me that Obedience is # 2 and not # 1. Every Physical body needs a Spiritual Foundation to stand or else that body is Dead. What affects many Christians, is a desire to find out things for themselves, after they were told what not to do, or what to stay away from; as in the case of Eve and Adam. What we need to remember is that God is our Father, therefore whatever He Tells us to keep away from, and what not to do, we need not seek to create a Mind of our own, because there is no other way but the way God Called us to follow, which leads to Life Everlasting. There is no other meaning to be a Christian, but to be a Servant that Truly TRUST IN THE LIVING GOD. And because we know the True meaning of the word Trust; we can say like the song writer "Where He may Lead me, I will go; because I have learnt to Trust Him so". We can joined Brother Job in his Testimony by saying:

"THOUGH HE SLAY ME, YET WILL I TRUST IN HIM". Job 13:15.

We can be like the Children of Israel that walked through the Red Sea, on Dry Land. If your Mind is not Inline / in agreement with God; then there is no way that you can Trust God; therefore you will never be Confident to Obey The Commands of God; because right there being out of Trust with God, you're not even sure that God can even Deliver you from the Mountain that is in front of you.

DISCIPLINE # 3. **PATIENCE TOWARDS GOD**: Now this is a subject that touches a lot of Christians heart, because we know that this is an area of our lives, that we have not yet got full control of.

The Bible encourages us in The Book of Psalms 27:14. "WAIT ON THE LORD: BE OF GOOD COURAGE, AND HE SHALL STRENGTHEN THINE HEART: WAIT, I SAY, ON THE LORD".

Isaiah 40:31 says: "BUT THEY THAT WAIT UPON THE LORD SHALL RENEW THEIR STRENGTH; THEY SHALL MOUNT UP WITH WINGS AS EAGLES; THEY SHALL RUN, AND NOT BE WEARY; AND THEY SHALL WALK, AND NOT FAINT".

It is hard at times to seek to understand exactly what God is Doing and when God is going to Accomplish that which He Says He is going to Do, especially in your personal life. I can tell you by experience, some of the times it becomes very frustrating, but just like what Asaph experience in Psalms 73. When he made mention of the prosperity of the wicked, he said his feet almost slipped, wondering if he had cleansed himself in vain; but then he said, he went into the House of God; then understood he the end of the wicked. My frustration continued until I gave spaced to myself to enter into Relationship with The Word of God; and it was in Relationship with God's Word, I discovered that when The Spirit of Patience is born in a Child of God life; it can only be compared to a word called PEACE. The Spirit of Patience Reveals that God is indeed THE ALPHA AND OMEGA; which is Revealed to be all the words of the Alphabet; thus manifesting that the Almighty God is The Living Word; that whatever position you may ever find yourself in; whatever Struggles, in whatever Darkness, facing whatever may be your Red Sea, or your High Mountain; the moment you acknowledge that you Trust and Believe in The God of Abraham, Isacc and Israel; that's the same moment that your God will identify a suitable Word within Himself, to Speak to your situation, that will allow your Mountains to disappear, like it wasn't even there.

Let us look on this for minute; How is it that we came to the realization as Christians, to understand that there is indeed A God? I can answer that question for you. One of the main medium through which we have identified that there is A God, is because someone invited us to Church and we heard The Words of God and believed; some of us was taught by our parents that God truly Exits and is to be Feared and Served; some of us by reading The Bible for ourselves, that's what brought the belief of God in our lives; some of us heard a Testimony, that was so Inspiring to our hearts that it brought forth a belief in our Minds that there is truly A God. But how many of us knows about God, because God has Revealed Himself Personally to us; now that's the Big, Big question! Have you ever asked yourself why it took Father Abraham twenty five (25) years for the Fulfillment / Foundation of his Blessing? If you should read very carefully the life and the story of Abraham; you would then realize that Abraham twenty five years after The Promise was made, was not the same Abraham when God first Spoke to him. Abraham went through a lot of Transitions / Transformation in his life, in order for him to reach a point and a discovery in his life, that he not only knew The Voice of God, but His life came to the level that he now knew The Presence of God even when everything was Dark. And that is what Patience is all about; allowing each and everyone one of God's Children to reach up to the Level that you actually know The God that you're Serving for yourself, and not by someone's Testimony.

It is important for me to let you know that in order for Patience to be born in your life; there must first be a satisfaction of Trust for God in your life. No Trust for God, results in no birth of The Spirit of Patience. Abraham got to the Level, which some of us could only dream, howbeit not impossible for us now, because of The Holy Ghost; when God told Abraham to offer his son for a sacrifice upon a Mountain; Abraham's response was willing to do whatever God Asked him to Do; The Bible Said Abraham thought to himself that God who Gave him the son from death, can without doubt bring back his son to life after he had killed him. How many of us reading this Message, have developed a Relationship with God, that goes beyond reading The Bible and going to Church, goes beyond Prayer and Fasting, and have now reached a level that you have heard The Voice of God calling for you in the night, just has how God was calling for Samuel while he sleepiest, in order to Communicate with him. For every Child of God, this is what God Needs to Develop in our lives;

an action of True Relationship from Father to Son and Sons of God to The Heavenly Father.

Patience is the only Medicine that can enable A Child of God to discover the birth of knowing The True Power of your God; through Patience the Physical man dies which enables the birth of The Spiritual man. The Spirit of Patience only works with God's Time and not man's time; man will always seek for a breakthrough when it pleases the flesh, but the Spiritual man through Patience is in Agreement with The Accepted Time of God which the Physical man can never understand. Through Patience only God Receive The Glory; and if it was up to man, God would never receive His Glory. Patience kills the enemy plans every time, because the enemy works with time, and seeks for God's People to complete that which he has tempt them with in a speedy time in order to catch The People of God in his snares; but God The Father Works in The Realms of Eternity, that confuse the enemy and allows the demons to tremble at every Presence of A Child of God that is born of The Spirit of Patience.

Note: whenever time you are asked to do something that requires haste, be very careful, because that spirit speaking to you might not be The Spirit of The Living God. There is one thing of fact that I need my Readers to understand, this is it: being A Child of God, we have got to understand that this Qualified State does not allow us to be immune from the voice of the Devil, in fact, what this Qualified State of being Sons of God cause, is for us to be Tempted and Tried even more than those who are not serving God. And because we are not immune from the voice of the Devil, we have got be very careful of the voices we hear, to make sure that we identify through these voices, The True Voice of The Living God. The Devil was able to speak to Eve, being then a creation of God which knew no sin; the Devil was able to speak to Cain, to kill his only brother that sucked the same breast he sucked, imagine! The Devil was able to speak to Achan, was able to speak to King Saul; the Devil was even able to speak to God when he asked permission in order to destroy Job's life; he was able to speak to Jesus Christ, The Lamb of God, tempting

God, seeking to let God bow down to his counsels and snares, of which The Lord Answered:

"Thou shalt not tempt the Lord thy God, and Him only shalt thou Serve".

Now if the Devil was able to come in the Realms of all these people and even God, what about me and you. Temptation is not sin, it's when you yield to the temptation. Each time the enemy looks on A Child of God that is born a Spiritual man, what he discover through his eyes is Eternity, no beginning and no ending, A Glory that he lost, which he can never receive again; then ironic, the Children of God ask the question, why is my cross so heavy to bear, why is the enemy at my heels in everything that I do; reason for this is because your destined to inherit that which he can no longer have, thus resulting in Jealousy and Envy; the devil now ensuring that he uses every tool to try and stop us from entering The Kingdom of God; and one of the main tool he seek to use, is the spirit of frustration, to make us want to give up or give in to his devices. If we could just look on the Cross which we bare as a duty and requirement for us to fulfill, then we would be fulfilling that which is required without realizing that the load is heavy. One of the main thing we learn in the World of work, is that once we love the work that were schedule to perform, no matter what the title of the job is, once we love our work, then the work becomes easy to do. What I'm encouraging Christians to do, is to love being A Child of God, no matter what comes; then, when we begin to love God's Word, we would then start to realize that we love doing what God Command us to fulfill, despite the challenges we face.

When we as Children of God has been Born Again and have learnt what it is to be Patient, then we would realize that our lives can never be out of time, as what the World would have us to believe, because even when this physical life has ended for a True Child of God, then it's just the right time for The Spiritual life to have full course. Paul said, to be absent from the flesh, is to be present in The Spirit. Let us take a look on this Table, which will better enable God's People to be a lot more patient. I testify and acknowledge that I sought the knowledge of those who are Experts in the field of Mathematics to bring forth the calculations of what you will discover in the table below.

GOD'S TIME / SPIRITUAL	MAN'S TIME / PHYSICAL
1. One thousand (1000) years equal	1. **One (1) day**
2. One (1) Day equals	2. **One thousand (1000) years**
3. **One (1) hour equals**	3. **41 years, 7 months, 27 days, 14 hours and 24 minutes.**
4. **One (1) minutes equal**	4. **8 months, 28 days, 19 hours and 12 minutes**
5. **One (1) second equals**	5. **4 days, 3 hours, 50 minutes and 24 second.**
6. **One (1) millisecond equals**	6. **6 minutes.**

Having come to the understanding of this table, I hope very much that there will be less impatient Christians; because the table reveals that most of us that just began Serving God for only five (5) years, would have resulting in our service, in God's Time of being only over six (6) minutes of service. Even those of us, that just began Serving God for only three (3) months, and would need God to give to us House, Car, Land, Job, Husband, Wife, Money, Wealth Etc. Not considering that we've but only completed twenty (20) seconds of Service in The Eyes of God. Look at this: many of God's People can't even pray pass one minute or five minutes, and then you look on the table and realize that we weren't even praying for one Millisecond in The Eyes of GOD; how serious are we about Prayer? There are Elements that seeks to bar our prayers from God, therefore an ordinary prayer at times is not sufficient. Bishop Austin Whitfield would say:

"THE PRAYER DIDN'T EVEN REACH THE ROOF OF THE CHURCH MUCH LESS TO REACH HEAVEN".

I'm not saying that the way to pray is only long prayers, but rather meaningful prayers that brings forth an effect. And you just imagine this, The Bible Said that Jesus Christ Prayed until His Sweat became as drops of blood. Now that's some prayer!

What about when our Pastor ask us to come together to observe a week of Fasting and Consecration Service; do you realize that we were asked to offer to God one and a half second (1 ½) of True Worship. And maybe it was that week of Service that God would have Moved our Mountains out of our lives.

Let us say we got a duty to perform in The Church, Namely being a Young People's President or being the Missionaries Director; and because we are human and have not yet been born unto Patience; after six (6) month or one (1) year we begin to get impatient and frustrated because there seems to be no growth or improvements. Not knowing that even when we have fulfilled one (1) earthly year of service, that is still just a little over one (1) minute of service in the Eyes and Realms of GOD. What if in God's Requirements, after a Child of God sows a seed, God's Required Time is five (5) Earthly years, which would be a little over six (6) minutes in The Eyes of God. I say what if; I do not know the time and the seasons that God have Destined for the Harvest of each seed that is sown by A Child of God. But if I were to give an answer as to the time it would take for the Harvest of A Child of God Blessing to be realized after the seed has been sowed, I would have to say three (3) to five (5) earthly years, by then God would have Fully Proven the fruit of the seed that was sown.

Ask yourself these questions:

1. Is God lacking of Understanding?
2. Is God in need of Knowledge?
3. Is Wisdom far from God?

This is what I'm trying to let us come to understand:
"GOD IS NOT STUPID"!
God is not going to Impart HIS **DIVINE BLESSING** on those

who are not yet Born Again, and their whole desire and life is set only to Please God; thus realizing the Fact, that the Harvest for the Child of God that have sown a Righteous seed, will take time to manifest, to prove that your desires and intentions are that of Righteousness. The Bible Says: St John 15:7.

"IF YE ABIDE IN ME, AND MY WORDS ABIDE IN YOU, YE SHALL ASK WHAT YE WILL, AND IT SHALL BE DONE UNTO YOU"

But The Lord never Said when it will be done. God Said Abide, and if I prove that you're abiding then I will bring forth the Harvest for you. Now if you're A Child of God that is always abiding, then whenever you call, there will be an immediate answer, because God has already Proven that you are a Son of GOD. A Miracle is however different, as it relies on the Individual who is the recipient of that Miracle; we can all receive a Miracle from GOD, only if we believe that God Can Do whatever we have put before Him to Do.

Psalms 37:7 Says: "REST IN THE LORD, AND WAIT PATIENTLY FOR HIM".

Take a look at this: For many of us, we spend years living in sin, becoming more and more corrupt by the minute; but then the opportunity came our way, for us to give over our lives unto God, but then, being now Servants of God, we expect that time will not be a factor for us to actually become clean; to reach to the Acceptable place that God Needs us to reach. Some of us baptized today, and next week, or next month or three months from now, we expect to reach to the highest level that God has in store for us. It doesn't work like that.

NOTE: PATIENCE IS A MUST IF YOU'RE SERVING GOD; THEREFORE LET US SEEK TO ALLOW THE SPIRIT OF PATIENCE TO BE BORN IN US.

DISCIPLINE # 4 IS TO LIFT UP A STANDARD FOR GOD BY COMING INTO RELATIONSHIP WITH GOD. Let me first share with you a secret; If your Relationship with God has not evolved to a place that it is considered to be SERIOUS, then God's Relationship with you will reflect exactly what you have put in that Relationship; that's the Truth.

The Bible said, "IF I BE LIFTED UP, THEN I WILL DRAW ALL MEN UNTO ME".

God is Searching for Serious Christians that are willing to uphold The Principles and Standards of who God is, thus enabling others to see The True Light of God in His People. Being in Relationship with God is a Child of God True Identity, without Relationship we are just another person that exist on this earth to make up the number that will stand before God at the Judgment Seat. We should not be happy going through this life and not seeking to find out who God Is. Look at the Irony, many of us that are Married, we spend so much time seeking to find out what pleases our Husbands and our Wives, what they like from what they dislike, if we should put forth the same energy that we have placed in our Relationship with our spouse towards God, what a beautiful Relationship we would have developed with our Saviour. There is one main thing that is necessary for us to understand in Relationship with God, and it is that, God comes First in everything, not second or third but FRIST; if you offer unto God second best, He will not accept it; ask Cain, ask the sons of Eli, ask Nadab and Abihu, ask King Saul, ask Achan, ask Ananias and Sapphira, all these story are a Testimony for us and for our Children's Children.

Proverb 3:5 & 6. Says: "TRUST IN THE LORD WITH ALL THINE HEART; AND LEAN NOT UNTO THINE OWN UNDERSTANDING. IN ALL THY WAYS ACKNOWLEDGE HIM, AND HE SHALL DIRECT THY PATHS".

The Bible Says in The Book of St Mark 8:34-38. "AND WHEN HE HAD CALLED THE PEOPLE UNTO HIM WITH HIS DISCIPLES ALSO, HE SAID UNTO THEM, WHOSOEVER WILL COME AFTER ME, LET HIM DENY HIMSELF, AND TAKE UP HIS CROSS AND FOLLOW ME. FOR WHOSOEVER WILL SAVE HIS LIFE SHALL LOSE IT; BUT WHOSOEVER SHALL LOSE HIS LIFE FOR MY SAKE AND THE GOSPEL'S, THE SAME SHALL SAVE IT. FOR WHAT SHALL IT PROFIT A MAN, IF HE SHALL GAIN THE WHOLE WORLD, AND LOSE HIS OWN SOUL? OR WHAT SHALL A MAN GIVE IN EXCHANGE FOR HIS SOUL? WHOSOEVER THEREFORE SHALL

BE ASHAMED OF ME AND OF MY WORDS IN THIS ADULTEROUS AND SINFUL GENERATION; OF HIM ALSO SHALL THE SON OF MAN BE ASHAMED, WHEN HE COMETH IN THE GLORY OF HIS FATHER WITH THE HOLY ANGELS".

Each Child of God should and must consider themselves to be A Light House for God, A Watch Man against every works of darkness; whenever we discover that darkness is trying to strangle light, which it can't, but darkness at time seeks to creep in our Marriage relationship, creep in our Family, creep in our Conversations and also seeks to creep in The Church of The Living God. We have got to stand upon The True Light of God. The Bible Said: Proverb 14:34.

"RIGHTEOUSNESS EXALTETH A NATION: BUT SIN IS A REPROACH TO ANY PEOPLE".

The Bible also made mention in The Book of Isaiah Chapter 5:20-25. Some of the Word says: "WOE UNTO THEM THAT CALL EVIL GOOD, AND GOOD EVIL; THAT PUT DARKNESS FOR LIGHT, AND LIGHT FOR DARKNESS; THAT PUT BITTER FOR SWEET, AND SWEET FOR BITTER! Verse 23 Says: WHICH JUSTIFY THE WICKED FOR REWARD, AND TAKE AWAY THE RIGHTEOUSNESS OF THE RIGHTEOUS FROM HIM! Verse 24 Says: THEREFORE AS THE FIRE DEVOURETH THE STUBBLE, AND THE FLAME CONSUMETH THE CHAFF, SO THEIR ROOT SHALL BE AS ROTTENNESS, AND THEIR BLOSSOM SHALL GO UP AS DUST: BECAUSE THEY HAVE CAST AWAY THE LAW OF THE LORD OF HOSTS, AND DESPISED THE WORD OF THE HOLY ONE OF ISRAEL".

Each time we walk out of our homes, the meditation should be to always ensure that we are The Light of the World, we should always be focused and inspired to do the right things at all times. Remember to just Lift Up God and God will Lift you Up. There is one thing I must mention, Bishop Austin Whitfield always asked the Church this Question:

"WHENEVER SOMEONE ASK YOU A QUESTION THAT THEY NEED THE TRUTH, AND YOU FAIL TO GIVE THEM THE TRUTH, BISHOP WOULD SAY, WHAT CAN THEY DO TO YOU IF YOU TELL THEM THE TRUTH, IF THEY WANT TO KILL YOU FOR THE TRUTH,

REJOICE BECAUSE YOU KNOW THAT YOU'RE NOT PLEASING MAN BUT INSTEAD YOU'RE PLEASING THE LIVING GOD".

Have a look at this scripture found in Psalms 94:16. "WHO WILL RISE UP FOR ME AGAINST THE EVILDOERS? OR WHO WILL STAND UP FOR ME AGAINST THE WORKERS OF INIQUITY"? Children of God, The Lord is asking us to Stand Up for Him.

DISCIPLINE # 5 IS SEPARATION. An easy way to describe the word Separation is a word that is called HOLINESS. Once we are Holy, there is no way we can mix with darkness; must be different. We must Walk different, Talk different, Look different and most important we must Feel different. It is the feeling of change that cause True Christians to hold unto their Faith, even when that Faith seems to be dying. One of the hardest thing to convince The Children of God with, is the Fact that you have to be Separated in order to remain on a Saved pathway. Yes, you're experiencing what it feels like to be Saved, but if there is not a Separation, then in the near future you will not remain Saved. Separation is speaking about a New Life, a different walk from what everyone else is doing, because Salvation is Personal, each person have got to make sure that they are sure that they are standing on Holiness. Therefore the Old Life along with the habits and attitude has no more place among the New Life. The Pastor or Bishop of The Church cannot be separated for a Believer, neither can The Missionaries or Ministers, Deacons, Brother and Sisters; each person has to stand on their two feet to answer the Call of Holiness. I'm going to allow The Bible to be the Main Speaker on this part of the Topic, that we can be convinced that this is God's Commandment. 2 Corinthians 5:17 says:

"THEREFORE IF ANY MAN BE IN CHRIST, HE IS A NEW CREATURE: OLD THINGS ARE PASSED AWAY; BEHOLD, ALL THINGS ARE BECOME NEW".

There are still other Scripture that can be given to strengthen this Message, they are as follows: 2 Corinthians 6:14-18. Apart of this Scripture Says:

"WHEREFORE COME OUT FROM AMONG THEM, AND BE YE SEPARATE, SAITH THE LORD, AND TOUCH NOT THE UNCLEAN

THING; AND I WILL RECEIVE YOU, AND WILL BE A FATHER UNTO YOU, AND YE SHALL BE MY SONS AND DAUGHTERS, SAITH THE LORD ALMIGHTY".

1 Corinthians 3:16 speaks about The Children of God being The Temple of God, in which The Spirit of God Dwells. 1 Corinthians 6:15 speaks about the members of our bodies not being ours anymore but now it is the members of Christ; making the emphasis that we cannot do what we feel like doing with God's Body.

1 CORINTHIANS 10:20-22 SAYS: "YE CANNOT DRINK THE CUP OF THE LORD, AND THE CUP OF DEVILS: YE CANNOT BE PARTAKERS OF THE LORD'S TABLE, AND OF THE TABLES OF DEVILS".

Romans 6:1&2 says: "WHAT SHALL WE SAY THEN? SHALL WE CONTINUE IN SIN, THAT GRACE MAY ABOUND? GOD FORBID. HOW SHALL WE, THAT ARE DEAD TO SIN, LIVE ANY LONGER THEREIN"?

Romans 12:1 says: "I BESEECH YOU THEREFORE, BRETHREN, BY THE MERCIES OF GOD, THAT YE PRESENT YOUR BODIES A LIVING SACRIFICE, HOLY, ACCEPTABLE UNTO GOD, WHICH IS YOUR REASONABLE SERVICE".

1 Peter 1:13-21. Apart of this Scripture Says: "BUT AS HE WHICH HATH CALLED YOU IS HOLY, SO BE YE HOLY IN ALL MANNER OF CONVERSATION; BECAUSE IT IS WRITTEN, BE YE HOLY; FOR I AM HOLY".

I cannot emphasize enough how important Holiness is to A Child of God; if we claim to be A Child of God, and there is no Holiness, then all we are, is just a big hypocrite. We are Crucifying Christ all over again; Holiness must become our watch word and life style. It is my advice to my Readers and I also made mention of this in The Church that I am responsible for; if you know that you're just not ready for Holiness, then take so time to gather yourself to accept The Responsibilities of being a Christian; then when you are truly ready, Christianity will become easy. Note: We can never become Holy if we choose to remain among Darkness, or Influence of Darkness. There is an exercise I often preform for The Church to explain the difference between Light and Darkness, between Holiness and

Unrighteousness. If you take half cup of oil and try to mix that oil with half cup of water, it doesn't matter how hard you attempt to mix, you could even use a Blender, once the mixture is settled, the oil molecules will return to its properties and the water molecules will remain by itself, the oil settling on the top, with the water settling at the bottom. That's what your Christian life is or should be; no matter how darkness tries to mix with us, because the ingredience that makes our life is Light, we just cannot be mixed, and when everything is settled we have to return to the place where Light is, and that is called Separation which is HOLINESS.

NOTE: Separation truly takes time to accomplish, it's not an overnight experience. And again I say being a Christian, Separation is a Must not a maybe. Christians can never see The Mighty Power Of God without Separation. Abraham was asked to separate himself from his kindred and his country, although being difficult to do it was something that he had to do in order to receive of God's Choice Blessing. Again if you read the Scriptures carefully, after separating himself from Lot his nephew, Abraham received another outpouring of blessing from God. Separation is not only done one time in your life, but Separation is a continuous process in a Child of God life; as we live, we will discover that the environment around us becomes temporal, thus the foundation of The True Light in you will always desire a New Experience of The Grace of God that only comes through Separation, which is Holiness. There is always Higher Heights in God, there is always a New and Fresh Revelation, there is always an Anointing that we have not yet experienced, but we cannot achieve this new level unless there is Holiness / Separation. Let us now look at ourselves in the mirror, and then we will realize that the new experience that we need from God is only being stopped by us, because we refuse to do the Separation; and don't tell God that you can't, because it will be interpreted that you just won't try to be Separated. Learn this: God will never come down to our level, we have got to climb the ladder of Holiness to reach up to God's Standards. If God Sees that we are trying to climb, then He will Give us a helping Hand.

Isaiah 55:8-11 a part of this Scripture Says: "FOR MY THOUGHTS ARE NOT YOUR THOUGHTS, NEITHER ARE YOUR WAYS MY WAYS, SAITH THE LORD. FOR AS THE HEAVENS ARE HIGHER THAN THE EARTH, SO ARE MY WAYS HIGHER THAN YOUR WAYS, AND MY THOUGHTS THAN YOUR THOUGHTS".

One of the biggest Separation a Child of God could ever feel; no it's not the lost of a Child or Parents or Friends or even Husbands or Wives; this is the Separation from God; we are calling, but it seems to be that God is far off; we cry for help and we are greeted with distance, then we sought The Lord and ask the question why Lord why; then The Lord Answered by telling us to read Isaiah 59:1&2. Which says:

"BEHOLD, THE LORD'S HAND IS NOT SHORTENED, THAT IT CANNOT SAVE; NEITHER HIS EAR HEAVY, THAT IT CANNOT HEAR: BUT YOUR INIQUITIES HAVE SEPARATED BETWEEN YOU AND YOUR GOD, AND YOUR SINS HAVE HID HIS FACE FROM YOU, THAT YE WILL NOT HEAR".

It is only then we get to realize the importance of being cleansed, of being different, of being Separated unto Holiness; we then realize that without Holiness no man shall see God nor receive of God's Attention whenever we are in trouble. The quicker we realize that Holiness is our Friend and only Friend; then we will realize what it means to be called God's Anointing. Remember this: GOD'S DIVINE BLESSING WILL NEVER BE REVEALED UNLESS THERE IS COMPLETE SEPARATION / HOLINESS.

DISCIPLINE # 6. THIS IS SPIRITUAL UNCLEANNESS THAT COMES IN THE FORM OF:

A. Perverseness.   B. Enchantments.   C. Divination.

Let us have a look on these three (3) Practices individually, so that we can fully understand the meaning of these words to know what to stay away from.

PERVERSENESS

According to the Webster's Dictionary, this word is coming from the word Perverse or to be perverse, which means willfully determined not to do what is expected or desired; to turn away from what is right, good, and proper. A wicked or corrupt person; a contrary person. For an Example: Jonah, after being told what do, he willfully and was determined not to do what God Command him to Do.

ENCHANTMENTS

This word is coming from the word Enchant, which means to subject to magical influence; placed under a spell or to place another person under a spell; to bewitch a person or to be in a position that you cause yourself to be bewitched. Enchantments practices is otherwise known as the Mother Woman or Obeah Man. And not only these persons are guilty, but also those who seek the services of these persons. A mark for unrighteousness is placed over that person's life and even over the life of their Children to come.

DIVINATION

This is the practice of seeking to foretell future events or to discover hidden knowledge by means of supernatural means, apart from The Presence and Will of God. This is done by means of spirits and demonic practices such as Sorcerers, Necromancers and witches; the story of King Saul going to a witch to bring Samuel from the death best describe the word Divination. 1 Samuel Chapter 28. It is important for us to understand that we don't have to be the person that is practicing these device, but only to be in the company of those who do it, and have pleasure in them that perform these act, by this The Bible Said that we are guilty of the same punishment as the doer, which is death. Then we can ask ourselves the question: How is it that the world, with all the television programs, why are they insisting on teaching us that witches, demonic forces, falling Angel and other Abominable things are accepted; when all it is teaching us is to get further away from God and cause us to only lose our Blessing that God has Given to us!

DISCIPLINE # SEVEN (7): Is a word that is well known, it is called **REST**. This discipline is to allow the Spiritual part of our life to have a day that it can refuel itself by coming to the Source of all strength. In The Bible it is called the Sabbath, of which some of us observe our Sabbath on a Saturday, while some of us observe this Rest on a Sunday. I'm not here to tell you what day should be your Sabbath, I'm rather demonstrating the importance of having a day that is set aside for God and His Word, that will bring forth a refreshment of your Soul; a day in which we come into The House of God to learn more about God, thus keeping our Spiritual life healthy.

"BECAUSE MAN SHALL NOT LIVE BY BREAD ONLY, BUT BY EVERY WORD THAT PROCEEDETH OUT OF THE MOUTH OF THE LORD DOTH MAN LIVE". Deuteronomy 8:3.

Then we wonder to ourselves why is it that many members that were Baptized and Serving God, are now not Serving God; here is the answer, the Disciplines are not being observed, therefore we are not on The Foundation, which means we must fall. Note: if you take your time to read The Book of Numbers Chapter 22- Chapter 24, you will identify this fact, at whatever time the enemy came up to destroy The People of God, even though they offered sacrifice to God; God's Response to Balaam was that He couldn't destroy Israel because they are Blessed and God didn't find any cause in Israel, that would cause Him to Destroy His People. But the very moment Israel walked out of The Will of God, The Presence of God could no longer abide with His People because sin was now present. The moment we walk out of The Will of God, we are no longer considered to be God's People, and that's a Fact. The Lord Said to Moses whenever the Children of Israel sinned; Moses go and talk to your people; but when the Children of Israel was doing God's Will, God Said:

"YE ARE A ROYAL PRIESTHOOD, HOLY NATION AND PECULIAR PEOPLE".

Therefore let this Message be a Testimony to us, as long as we keep in The Will of God, there is nothing the enemy can do to cause God to turn away The Divine Blessing that He has Destined over our lives. We are only recognize as being a Blessing if we continue to do what God Command us to Fulfill. NOTE: If we have received of God's Blessing and are not determine to work on these Disciplines to ensure that we keep God's Blessings; then it is sad to say, but we are going to find ourselves losing God's Blessing.

I love God too much to fail Him now. I hope this Message has been an Inspiration to all my Readers; my continual joy is to know that these Messages are helping God's People to lift up a higher standard for God. May The Lord Jesus Christ continue to Bless, Inspire and continue to Direct your Life, continue to pray for my strength that I will be able to do that which God would have me to do, which is to Inspire God's People. From The Servant of God and The Ministry of The Church of Jesus Christ Fellowship; God Bless you. Pastor Lerone Dinnall.

THE SEVEN DISCIPLINES TO OBSERVE, THE SECRET OF HOW TO REMAIN BLESSED...

THE TEST; ARE
YOU READY?

Message # 74   Date Started June 20, 2017
                                Date Finalized, June 22 2017.

JOB CHAPTER 1:6-12. "NOW THERE WAS A DAY WHEN THE SONS OF GOD CAME TO PRESENT THEMSELVES BEFORE THE LORD, AND SATAN CAME ALSO AMONG THEM. AND THE LORD SAID UNTO SATAN, WHENCE COMEST THOU? THEN SATAN ANSWERED THE LORD, AND SAID, FROM GOING TO AND FRO IN THE EARTH, AND FROM WALKING UP AND DOWN IN IT. AND THE LORD SAID UNTO SATAN, HAST THOU CONSIDERED MY SERVANT JOB, THAT THERE IS NONE LIKE HIM IN THE EARTH, A PERFECT AND AN UPRIGHT MAN, ONE THAT FEARETH GOD, AND ESCHEWETH EVIL? THEN SATAN ANSWERED THE LORD, AND SAID, DOTH JOB FEAR GOD FOR NOUGHT? HAST NOT THOU MADE AN HEDGE ABOUT HIM, AND ABOUT HIS HOUSE, AND ABOUT ALL HE HATH ON EVERY SIDE? THOU HAST BLESSED THE WORK OF HIS HANDS, AND HIS SUBSTANCE IS INCREASED ON THE LAND. BUT PUT FORTH

THINE HAND NOW, AND TOUCH ALL THAT HE HATH, AND HE WILL CURSE THEE TO THY FACE. AND THE LORD SAID UNTO SATAN, BEHOLD, ALL THAT HE HATH IS IN THY POWER; ONLY UPON HIMSELF PUT NOT FORTH THINE HAND. SO SATAN WENT FORTH FROM THE PRESENCE OF THE LORD".

Job Chapter 2:1-8. "AND THERE WAS A DAY WHEN THE SONS OF GOD CAME TO PRESENT THEMSELVES BEFORE THE LORD. AND THE LORD SAID UNTO SATAN, FROM WHENCE COMEST THOU? AND SATAN ANSWERED THE LORD, AND SAID, FROM GOING TO AND FRO IN THE EARTH, AND FROM WALKING UP AND DOWN IN IT. AND THE LORD SAID UNTO SATAN, HAST THOU CONSIDERED MY SERVANT JOB, THAT THERE IS NONE LIKE HIM IN THE EARTH, A PERFECT AND AN UPRIGHT MAN, ONE THAT FEARETH GOD, AND ESCHEWETH EVIL? AND STILL HE HOLDETH FAST HIS INTEGRITY, ALTHOUGH THOU MOVEDST ME AGAINST HIM, TO DESTROY HIM WITHOUT CAUSE. AND SATAN ANSWERED THE LORD, AND SAID, SKIN FOR SKIN, YEA, ALL THAT A MAN HATH WILL HE GIVE FOR HIS LIFE. BUT PUT FORTH THINE HAND NOW, AND TOUCH HIS BONE AND HIS FLESH, AND HE WILL CURSE THEE TO THY FACE. AND THE LORD SAID UNTO SATAN, BEHOLD HE IS IN THINE HAND; BUT SAVE HIS LIFE. SO WENT SATAN FORTH FROM THE PRESENCE OF THE LORD, AND SMOTE JOB WITH SORE BOILS FROM THE SOLE OF HIS FOOT UNTO HIS CROWN. AND HE TOOK HIM A POTSHERD TO SCRAPE HIMSELF WITHAL; AND HE SAT DOWN AMONG THE ASHES".

St Luke Chapter 4:1-13. "AND JESUS BEING FULL OF THE HOLY GHOST RETURNED FROM JORDAN, AND WAS LED BY THE SPIRIT INTO THE WILDERNESS, BEING FORTY DAYS TEMPTED OF THE DEVIL. AND IN THOSE DAYS HE DID EAT NOTHING: AND WHEN THEY WERE ENDED, HE AFTERWARDS HUNGERED. AND THE DEVIL SAID UNTO HIM, IF THOU BE THE SON OF GOD, COMMAND THIS STONE THAT IT BE MADE BREAD. AND JESUS ANSWERED HIM, SAYING, IT IS WRITTEN, THAT MAN SHALL NOT LIVE BY BREAD ALONE, BUT BY EVERY WORD OF GOD. AND THE DEVIL, TAKING HIM UP INTO AN HIGH MOUNTAIN, SHEWED

UNTO HIM ALL THE KINGDOMS OF THE WORLD IN A MOMENT OF TIME. AND THE DEVIL SAID UNTO HIM, ALL THIS POWER WILL I GIVE THEE, AND THE GLORY OF THEM: FOR THAT IS DELIVERED UNTO ME; AND TO WHOMSOEVER I WILL I GIVE IT. IF THOU THEREFORE WILT WORSHIP ME, ALL SHALL BE THINE. AND JESUS ANSWERED AND SAID UNTO HIM, GET THEE BEHIND ME, SATAN: FOR IT IS WRITTEN, THOU SHALT WORSHIP THE LORD THY GOD, AND HIM ONLY SHALT THOU SERVE. AND HE BROUGHT HIM TO JERUSALEM, AND SET HIM ON A PINNACLE OF THE TEMPLE, AND SAID UNTO HIM, IF THOU BE THE SON OF GOD, CAST THYSELF DOWN FROM HENCE: FOR IT IS WRITTEN, HE SHALL GIVE HIS ANGELS CHARGE OVER THEE, TO KEEP THEE: AND IN THEIR HANDS THEY SHALL BEAR THEE UP, LEST AT ANY TIME THOU DASH THY FOOT AGAINST A STONE. AND JESUS ANSWERED SAID UNTO HIM, IT IS SAID, **THOU SHALT NOT TEMPT THE LORD THY GOD.** AND WHEN THE DEVIL HAD ENDED ALL THE TEMPTATION, HE DEPARTED FROM HIM FOR A SEASON".

I Honor, Praise and Magnify The Ever Faithful God, Jesus Christ The Lamb of God. It is Truly a pleasure for me to be able to be in this Position, yet another time, to Magnify God, through the means of writing Inspired Messages for both My Family and The Church Family.

Things that we consider to be Real is not necessarily those things that are placed before our eyes for each day. The Lord Revealed that, that which is Real, is that which Last and Out Last everything that we should experience in this life being Physical. With that being said; this example gives us the Understanding to realize that the only thing a Child of God will ever experience in this life as being Real, is God, and everything that God has Freely Given to all those who TRUST HIM. This explanation serves the purpose of allowing each and every Individual that is Serving God, to come into the belief and Understanding to acknowledge that every Test that is formed, that will ever be formed, is **NOT REAL,** but in Fact, only a design to allow the Sons of God to reach the Continual Higher Level in God.

And to explain Not Real, I'm not saying that you will not Physically, Spiritually and Emotionally experience the Test; but rather what I'm trying to let my Readers understand, is that every Test that is destined for a Child of God, it's only designed is to build The Spiritual Man, then after The Spiritual Man has overcome that which was just a Test; then it is now immediately realized that the Test just came for a Season and a time in your life to fulfill just a small purpose in your life.

After passing that Test, you'll now find yourself looking back on that very Test, and wonder if it was really that Test that caused you to lose your night sleep. The Test becomes the State of Not Real because you've now pass the Level and the Process to overcome that Test; therefore it bears no more effect on your life. And don't worry, because this Christian walk is completely filled with a walk of Testing; therefore a Child of God can never become comfortable, because as soon as one Test is finished, there will be another Test that is on the way.

It is important to explain to my Readers, that if you're not a Child of God, you will not be given the opportunity to sit this Test. Because only Children of God are Placed Worthy to take the Test; because at the end of each Test, there is unveil one Step / Level of God's Divine Purpose and Movement within our lives. Therefore I'm sorry for those Christians that don't want to experience the Test. Now there are many that is in The Church, and is also a part of The Church; but this Test is not for everyone that is wearing a Title, but rather for those who are The Tithes of The Lord, to enable that God Can Bring His People to a state of Perfection. Those who are not Serving God is not eligible to take the Test, nor will they experience what the Test is like, rather those who are not Serving God, will experience the repercussion of their Actions or the Sinful life that they are living, and at the end of the day, they have no reward or scale falling from their eyes to reveal that which they are experiencing is not real, but to them it continues to be Real and Real every day that they live.

Now to Understand even clearly; when a Child of God is first faced with the Test, it then seems like a Mountain that is hard to climb; but when this Child of God begins to embrace the Test, it is now observed, that God has Placed stairs with railings on that Mountain, to make the journey of the Test becomes a lot easier than what it was first exposed to be. Then after climbing that Mountain with the Assistance from God, you'll find that you've overcome the Test without realizing that you've now reached the Top of the Mountain of that same Test.

There is a four (4) Process Mystery that has been Revealed to me regarding the Test that the Children of God must face, and it goes like this:

T: Temptation :- One of the first process of each Test is to identify exactly, the type of Material that makes up each Child of God. Now many that desires to Serve God, has the earnest expectation that they can perform for God, but at the same time, we are missing the Foundational Ingredience, that being The Spirit of God; which if it is not in full Operation in The Temple in which it is dwelling, then that person will not be able to fulfill the firm Requirement of Pleasing God in Spirit and in Truth. Temptation is not desirable, but it's one of the main medium through which God can Identify who is capable to withstand the different levels of environment that does exist in the work for God.

"THERE HATH NO TEMPTATION TAKEN YOU BUT SUCH AS IS COMMON TO MAN: BUT GOD IS FAITHFUL, WHO WILL NOT SUFFER YOU TO BE TEMPTED ABOVE THAT YE ARE ABLE; BUT WITH THE TEMPTATION ALSO MAKE A WAY TO ESCAPE, THAT YE MAY BE ABLE TO BEAR IT". 1 Corinthians Chapter 10:13.

Each Child of God has to go through the Temptation to determine whether or not their Sacrifice for God is True or it is Vain; therefore the life of a Child of God has to be Tested by first the World, to prove that the confession of our Soul is indeed Faithful to The King of kings and The Lord of lords, Jesus Christ The Lamb of God. Then after that Child of God has passed the Temptation to surpass the Elements and Environment of the World, it is now time for that Child of God to be Tempted / Tested by The Church and the Brethren that are in The Church; because it must be identify that, that which causes also the other members in a Church to strive for Excellence is the Fact that, when a True Child of God is Tried and Tempted by the World and then The Church, and the Revelation of those Test would have Manifested Pure Gold, it is taken note of, and then others in The Church would then realize that there is a member that is a part of The Body of Christ that is 100% Genuine; this stirs the pot, to allow others to now become jealous, in desiring also to become a Genuine Christian; this is known as iron sharpening iron. After this the Child of God is exposed to one final Temptation / Test, that being of The Word of God; this meaning that the undiluted Word, which is God, has to examine carefully, every Child of God to determine that such an Individual, their Foundation is in Fact The Solid Rock. Therefore that Child of God is now Tried Word for Word to ensure that The Word that is God, is not only in The Bible, but it has now found itself to be Living in The Temple of that Child of God, a Holy Temple for The Spirit of God to Remain.

E : Emotional Transformation :- There will become times in each Test that is Faced, that a Child of God will experience the Transformation of how they looked on God; because one of the first thing that is observed by each Child of God, is to look on God has being a Father at all times; but the Fact still remains, that we are so far away from God, that at any given time, even in Church, and although we have Received the Gift of The Holy Ghost, if we have not yet experience the Fullness of The Holy Ghost, then that which we experience from God, is but just a little fraction of what The Full Presence of God would or should allow us to experience. With that being said, a Child of God is always on a Ladder to climb up towards the Expectation and Requirements of that which God Demands for us to be. Therefore because God is our Father; at times when it is required that we must climb, and while climbing there are certain things we would desire to retain, these are the things that God is Seeking first to strip from our Circle; because Divine Relationship with God does not include Physical Attachments and Sentiments. So then, it is with this Mindset that God begins in the process of the Test to strip, and it is when we are being stripped, there arise an Emotional Transformation of how we first looked on God. At first God is our Loving Father, who will never Do anything to hurt us; now while experiencing the Test, it is like God becomes our enemy; because everything that is being removed, we then look to the Heavens to ask God why is He Allowing all these things to happen, and when you look around, it seems to be that you are the only one that is experiencing what you are experiencing; and it is with this state of Mind, if you do not understand what God is Doing, you will remain in a state of depression, and now saying to yourself and to God, WHY ME, WHY ME? But then if we could just listen carefully to The Voice of God, we will then hear God Saying, "WHY NOT YOU; ARE YOU NOT MARKED AND DESTINED FOR GREAT WORKS; WITH GREAT WORKS COMES GREAT RESPONSIBILTY AND GREAT SACRIFICE". The sooner we identify that the Test is to make us Great, the better we will be able to embrace each challenge of the Test. Remember that during this process of stripping, **NEVER TO CURSE GOD;** but rather be like Job, and say: "THE LORD GIVETH, THE LORD TAKETH AWAY, BLESSED BE THE NAME OF THE LORD".

S: Spiritual Separation :- There comes a time after each training of Individuals, that such an individual or Child of God will and must be left alone, that you will wonder if you even had a Relationship with The Father. There is the earnest desire by yourself to do everything that is customary for you to do, that previously allowed you to feel The Presence of The Almighty God; but although you Fasted and Prayed; you Worshipped and spend time to read your Bible, with all this being done, there is the clear evidence that The Spirit of God is nowhere to be felt. Then we start to wonder, what is it that we have done so bad to allow not even the Movement of The

Anointing of God to Acknowledge that He is still here. If we could just see to understand all that we need to understand in The Spiritual, then we will be fully knowledgeable of each and every process that The Lord is Allowing us to go through. Because it is Revealed by God that because a Child of God that is Destined for a purpose, has to climb the Ladder of Spirituality; The Lord then makes it to be very uncomfortable for that Child of God to remain in the position that, that Child of God now finds themselves to be comfortable in, therefore the old Level has to be killed, and the only way that The Lord can demonstrate to us that we have lived out our purpose on that Level, is to move The Spiritual Man that is inside of us to The Higher Level, therefore starving us of the simple Touch of The Spirit Man, to allow us to identify that there is a need for us to get to a Higher Level in God. Each Child of God has got to understand that despite of the different challenges that comes with the Test; each Test is designed to bring forth a Higher Level in The Spirit Man.

T: Time To Die :- Now the Completion of each Test will never be completed unless the Old Man of the Old Level is put to rest, meaning that the Old Man with his characters and desires, and way of doing things is no more. Then after it is realized by God that there is now no more Old Man / Physical Man; it is with this evidence that the Child of God will experience the embracing of a Higher Level in The Spirit Man, with New Desires, New Characteristics, New Office, New Position and also New Revelations. It is then realized by everyone else that the old person who you were is no more, and even if someone comes to you, seeking for you to go back to the character and desire of the Old Man, they will now realize from you that there is absolutely no desire or intention for the New Man to go back and dig up the Old Man. It is after the Child of God has experience death, that this Child of God will appreciate the Test that The Lord Allowed them to go through. Because without the Test there can be no Death, it is the characteristics of the Test that is design for each Child of

God, to allow the Old Man to be no more. If not so, then what is the reason and purpose of the Test?

Is there a confusing spirit in us to think that God Delights in Seeing His Children Suffer? But rather, by the means of Suffering, this event put to death every Character of the Old Man; therefore Suffering by means of The Test is one of God's Main Tool. And if when the Test is over and we have now been Strengthen in The Spirit Man; then that experience of the Test that a Child of God would have to go through is spelt these words: **THE LOVE OF A FATHER.**

Now let me repeat; every Child of God that is Destined to have a Purpose for The Ministering of The Kingdom of God, that Child of God has a Test with their name on it, which is completely FIXED by God to ensure that every Character of the Old Man is completely Dead. Therefore a person that is enduring their Test, if they are not knowledgeable of what to expect in the Test; that Child of God may and will endure a long Season facing that one Test; therefore not coming to the realization and understanding that God Brought the Test to kill the Flesh. Because no flesh can Glory in The Presence of God. Therefore for those who sees a fellow Child of God enduring their Test, don't be quick to judge, because each person that goes through the Test will lose their way of thinking, they will even behave in a way that is completely out of Character, because that Old Character has to Die. And don't worry about those who boast themselves, and have not yet experience the Test, because when it is time for that person to face the Test, if they are Destined for Ministry, they will then realize that boasting is Vain, and also a Character that has to be Killed to past the Test to reach The Higher Level in God.

Note: Always remember that whatever God has Destined for a Child of God to face for their Test, just remember that it doesn't take away from being what it is; that being JUST A TEST. When it has ended it will pass away.

This Message is based on my life experience of the Test that I faced, and the different Categories of that Test. I hope and pray, that through reading this Message, the Future Generation will be able to have a clearer understanding of what is the TEST; and for those in The Church, that we will be able to grow from strength to strength through this Revelation that God Has Given.

I Honor, Praise and Magnify The Ever Faithful God, Jesus Christ, The Lamb of God. Continue to offer a Continual Prayer for this Ministry and for My Family, In The Matchless Name of Jesus Christ.

THE TEST; ARE YOU READY?

TRUST IN GOD

Message # 43.   **Date Started January 3, 2017**
                                     Date Finalized January 5, 2017.

WHAT A MIGHTY GOD we Serve, Angels bow before Him, Heaven and Earth Adore Him, what a Mighty God we Serve! I Greet and Salute all My Father's Children in The Wonderful Saving Name Of Jesus Christ our Soon Coming King. As always, this opportunity is a Blessing for me to be in this Position to Represent God. It is fitting that the year 2017 be started with a Message of this Caliber; considering that the Times and the Seasons of life has been significantly altered; not that those who are Serving God is surprised by the events that are taking place in the World, but to actually see it Manifesting before our very eyes, makes us realize that the only thing left to do is just to look up because our Redemption Draws nigh.

I went to Watch Evening Service which took place on the last day of the month of December 2016, not knowing what the Message would be, then The Lord Revealed the Message that should be Preached, and it was called, "TIME TO LOOK UP", taken from the book of St Matthew Chapter 24. After Presenting the Sermon, I realized that the year coming would be one that brings with it a lot of Challenges, thus the People of God have got to make sure that there is a lot of Faith and Trust in God, to ensure that we are able to Survive, and don't forget the use of Wisdom; and if it is God's Will that we are Tested beyond that which we are able to Survive, then we must have the full Assurance to know for a fact that our True Home is in Heaven Above. I am aware that it is mentioned in The Bible that God will not put more on us than that which we are able to bare, regarding Temptation; God will Provide a way for us to escape. 1 Corinthians 10:13. But we must also remember that The Bible Says Perilous times will come, and with Perilous times, there will no Doubt be increased Temptations and Trials. Perilous times are now Here!

The Bible Encourage us that we must Pray without ceasing; 1 Thessalonians 5:17. The Bible also ask that we walk circumspectly, not as fools, but as wise, Redeeming the time, because the days are evil; Ephesians 5:15&16. Colossians 4:5 says:

"WALK IN WISDOM TOWARDS THEM THAT ARE WITHOUT, REDEEMING THE TIME".

The Lord Spoke to us in The Book of St John Chapter 14:1-3. Which says: "LET NOT YOUR HEART BE TROUBLED: YE BELIEVE IN GOD, BELIEVE ALSO IN ME. IN MY FATHER'S HOUSE ARE MANY MANSIONS: IF IT WERE NOT SO, I WOULD HAVE TOLD YOU. I GO TO PREPARE A PLACE FOR YOU. AND IF I GO AND PREPARE A PLACE FOR YOU, I WILL COME AGAIN, AND RECEIVE YOU UNTO MYSELF; THAT WHERE I AM, THERE YE MAY BE ALSO".

This is one of the Greatest Consolation that was ever recorded in The Bible, to allow God's People to have the Confidence of a Hope that will never fail; no matter what this world takes away from us, this hope remains firm within the Minds and Heart of God's Chosen Vessels. As we step into a New Year, not really knowing what to expect exactly; but it is important for us as Christians to be Steadfast and Unmovable in the Faith, upholding A Undiluted Trust for God and His Promises for our lives; and also with the reminder that we need to live each day anticipating if this is the day that the Trumpet Of The Lord will Sound.

Saints, believe me, the World has gotten so vile, that we just don't know what to expect anymore; the World at present is studying the lives of Christians to see how much pressure they can put us under, to make us crack under the pressure that they have manufactured for our lives; the days that the Egyptian placed Task Masters upon the Children of Israel, to pressure them, that they should die, is now being repeated. But there is a Secret to the pressure that we face; it will not make us worse, but instead it will allow us to reach the QUALIFIED STATE of being JUSTIFIED BEFORE GOD. There is one thing that we need to remember: The Word of God is the TRUE FOUNDATION of everything that ever was, that is present now, and that will ever exist; therefore if we are living in the Foundation of God which is The Living Word, then whatever pressure comes our way, we will be able to stand the Test, because the True Material would have been found in us.

The Three Hebrew Boys Namely: Shadrach, Meshach and Abednego, was put to the Test, and while the punishment became seven times more than what it should be, they did not shake, wasn't worried, but they boldly looked in the eyes of King Nebuchadnezzar and said: "O KING NEBUCHADNEZZAR, WE ARE NOT CAREFUL TO ANSWER THEE IN THIS MATTER. IF IT BE SO, OUR GOD WHOM WE SERVE IS ABLE TO DELIVER US FROM THE BURNING FIERY FURNACE, AND HE WILL DELIVER US OUT OF THINE HAND, O KING. BUT IF NOT, BE IT KNOWN UNTO THEE, O KING, THAT WE WILL NOT SERVE THY GODS, NOR WORSHIP THE GOLDEN IMAGE WHICH THOU HAST SET UP". Daniel Chapter 3.

We have read this story many times, but are we yet in that Position and Anointing that we are willing and able to Stand Up for God even if it is going to cost us our lives? The Topic says Trust in God; let us ask ourselves these questions: after reading The Bible for years, can we now say that we are in a Position that we Trust God? Going to Church for years and giving our Testimonies, do we Trust God? Not only saying these words from our mouth but our Character can bear witness to bring forth the Action that is necessary to Reveal a Great Trust in God!

The Lord Revealed to me that to Trust Him, is to Receive an Anointing that carries that person to another Level, which will allow that individual to STEP INTO THE UNKNOWN, and to be Confident that the very Unknown has No Power to hurt a Child of GOD, because the Unknown Represent the DWELLING PLACE OF THE MOST HIGH GOD; because having a Trust in God means that you haven't seen with your Physical eye what God is going to Do or how God is going to Provide. The Bible says in Psalms 121. "I WILL LIFT UP MINE EYES UNTO THE HILLS, FROM WHENCE COMETH MY HELP. MY HELP COMETH FROM THE LORD, WHICH MADE HEAVEN AND EARTH. HE WILL NOT SUFFER THY FOOT TO BE MOVED: HE THAT KEEPETH THEE WILL NOT SLUMBER. BEHOLD, HE THAT KEEPETH ISRAEL SHALL NEITHER SLUMBER NOR SLEEP. THE LORD IS THY KEEPER: THE LORD IS THY SHADE UPON THY RIGHT HAND. THE SUN SHALL NOT SMITE THEE BY DAY, NOR THE MOON BY NIGHT. THE LORD SHALL PRESERVE THEE FROM ALL EVIL: HE SHALL PRESERVE THY SOUL. THE LORD SHALL PRESERVE THY GOING OUT AND THY COMING IN FROM THIS TIME FORTH, AND EVEN FOR EVERMORE".

Trust; in many ways is to Believe God's Plan; and to believe God's Plan for our lives, is to believe in God's Timing for our Lives; that will not come when we are expecting it to come, but will instead be Manifested when there is the full Assurance that its only God that will Receive the Glory for what He has Done for our lives. When God has Fulfilled that which He say He is going to Fulfill, there will be an Impression that is left upon our lives that will force Gratitude from our Souls, to ensure that the Generation to come will know what God has Done, thus ensuring that there is always a future Generation that will no doubt continue to Lift Up the Name of Jesus Christ throughout all Generations.

According to the Webster's Dictionary, the word Trust means: Reliance on the integrity, strength, ability, surety, etc., of a person or thing; confidence. It went on to say that it also means: confident expectation of something; hope. If we should examine carefully the meaning of the word Trust, we will then identify that this interpretation speaks mainly to that which has been revealed to man, meaning physical; not that it is not helpful, because it serve a purpose for God's People to understand at least one level of Trust. The Lord Revealed to me, that for a Child of God to Truly Trust in God, that Trust has to be Tested with TIME AND FAILURE.

The Test of Time is as a result, that Trust is a Spirit, that is Required to Grow in the life of a Child of God, therefore if there is no Growth within the time of Service, there will be no Manifestation of Trust for God; Ten, Twenty or Fifty years going to Church, does not necessarily Manifest that a person has Grown in The Spirit of God; and I repeat, if there is no Growth, there will be no Trust. Note: Many Christians are still to understand that The QUALITY OF SERVICE, Climbs Higher and will always Out Shine the QUANTITY OF SERVICE. Quality represent Spirit, while Quantity represent Physical or Temporal. One will be heavy having a Foundation, while the other will be as feather to the wind. Quantity represent the House of Clay, while Quality represent The Spirit of God that dwells within that House. It is The Spirit that Quickeneth, the Flesh profited nothing. The big question to ask is: What have we done for God with our Lives for the quantity of the years we've been Serving God; was those years of Quality?

Let us look at the Test of Failure; this being that of our own strength; because God cannot Receive His Expected Glory based on the ability that man will have in his Mind, the taught to say that it was my strength that brought forth deliverance or success. Example of this action is that of King Nebuchadnezzar in The Book of Daniel Chapter 4:28-37.

When we think about it, we should really examine our Trust in God; is it that when we have received a Husband or a Wife, Children, House and Car, a Job, Positions and Opportunity; is it when things are good, at these times we lament the words, I Trust God! what about when things are very bad, when there is no food for days and we are forced to Fast, no work to support the bills and to take care of the mortgage or even the Family, a sickness that seems to be getting more worse than better, Husbands and Wives threatening to break the

Circle, lost your Job or Position in the work place, the Enemy comes in front of you with a Gun saying he's here to take our lives away and that of our Family; the Devil telling us what he's going to do to us; at that time, in that Atmosphere, will we be in a Position or an Anointing to Declare and to Decree that I TRUST GOD BECAUSE THAT TRUST IS NOW A PART OF WHO YOU ARE!

Will we have that type of Relationship with our God to know that even though we can't see not even a spot or peak of light, in that type of Darkness will we be the Light to Manifest the Foundation of the Trust that God need us to have in Him? Will we say like Job, though He Slay me, yet will I Trust Him. The Lord Revealed that because Trust for a Child of God is to step into the Unknown, it is Manifested that Trust in God is Completely Spiritual, and at times when we look to understand Spiritual, the Manifestation of Spiritual is the Darkest place to walk in, of which we don't know how long and deep the Darkness of uncertainty will last for; but finds that if we have Grown in God, the Darkness now become Comfortable. There is nothing physical about putting our Trust in God apart from the action that demonstrate that very Trust. Our Trust will never be Spiritual if it is that because we have seen some evidence that caused us to Trust; rather, the type of Trust that God Requires, is that of the Unknown Revelation. The only evidence we need to Trust, is The Living Word of God; The Word of God is more than Sufficient to allow God's Children to Believe even when the Atmosphere dictates that we should not Believe in God.

Trust in God means, I don't see God, but I know God is there, and He is Going to Work for me. Therefore if it is that we are exercising our Faith to Trust God, majority of the journey is going to be Dark, so Dark, that at times we may wonder if it is that we are on the right path of Trusting in God, or is it that we are completely driven Insane to follow a pathway that everyone else say, that there is no path on the road that we are travelling on. Each time we look on the words Trust in God, there must be the Confirmation in us to say; GOD KNOWS WHAT HE IS DOING.

There was a time in my life that I was constantly Asking God what is He going to Do for my life, what's the Plan? Because I just could not see the path that The Lord had me on. The Lord Responded by Saying:

"YOUR DUTY IS TO TRUST GOD, AND GOD'S DUTY IS TO BRING FORTH THE MANIFESTATION OF THAT TRUST".

We all need to understand that the reason why there is Great Blessings for God's People is because there is Great Trust; the reason for Great Deliverance is because there is a Great Relationship of Trust for those of us who are Servants for God. Have a look at Daniel, Great Relationship resulted in Great Works for God; Manifesting the Hidden Secrets that no Magicians or Astrologers or Wise men could Reveal; if we think about it, how can we Reveal God's Secret, if we are not found to be in The Unknown of God! Have a look at David; a man after God's own Heart, God Allowed him to have a Great Kingdom, considering that he wasn't even chosen to be at the Sacrifice. Have a look at Abraham, because of his Faith it was accounted to him for Righteousness which made him a Friend of God, that allowed all Nations that is to be Blessed, must be Blessed because of the Sacrifice of Abraham; Enoch couldn't see death because the Relationship was strong; Elijah was taken up by a Chariot of fire, his Relationship caused him not to taste death. GREAT RELATIONSHIP BRINGS FORTH GREAT TRUST, WHICH THEN BRINGS FORTH GREAT BLESSINGS.

What is our Relationship like with God? It's time to search. This answer to that question will Manifest the Measurement of the Trust that we have in God, and will also bring forth the measurement of the blessings that we must receive from God. One of the Biggest problem that exist in the lives of Children of God, is the Fact that we have not yet learned how to Trust God, and the cause for this is because there is not found in us a Strong Relationship with God; Relationship starts with believing that God Exist, then it moves on to that person taking up the Responsibility of needing to read The Word of God, to thus strengthen that Relationship; after believing and reading, then there is the Mission that we must begin to Live the Requirements of that which God Asked us to Accomplish; then after we've started to

Live, then the Revelation of Trust for God will be Realized; Trust in God now becomes a part of our daily routine, it becomes a part of us.

There are physical things that can help us to better understand Trust; if it is found that a person is generally afraid of the Dark, if that person stays in the Dark long enough, then that person will no longer be afraid of Darkness, because that Darkness will then be a part of that person's life, and that is what God Needs from us; God Need for us as Children of God to spend as much time that we can spend in His Words; in Fasting Services; in Prayer; and most important in living a Holy life that will Represent Him, then after we have done that, we will then realize that we are no more afraid of the Darkness of Trust, we are now comfortable in whatever Challenges of life that comes our way; because whatever comes, there is the Trust in us to realize that it is God that caused the day to be of the Darkness that it represents. And if God makes the path so dark, then the same God can Allow the Path to become Light, after we have learnt what it is that we should have learned in the Darkness, because the Darkness is only set to make us learn how to Trust in God. If we think about it, was not Light Manifested from Darkness, even though there was no evidence to support the Knowledge of Light beside that of God!

Genesis 1:1-3. "IN THE BEGINNING GOD CREATED THE HEAVEN AND THE EARTH. AND THE EARTH WAS WITHOUT FORM, AND VOID; AND DARKNESS WAS UPON THE FACE OF THE DEEP. AND THE SPIRIT OF GOD MOVED UPON THE FACE OF THE WATERS. AND GOD SAID, LET THERE BE LIGHT: AND THERE WAS LIGHT".

We have to believe that Trust in God will then demonstrate that after we have gone through the Darkest experience, then God will, from that Darkness, Declare and Decree in that Darkness, that it will now become Light for our Path. Some Darkness that we endure is called sickness; another Darkness may be Persecutions and Trials; some of us will face Famine and Nakedness, while some of us will face spiritual warfare, some will face and experience the loss of a love one, while some will face Rejection on every side. No matter what the Darkness is, God has Placed that Darkness in our Lives for us to get the victory of Light through that Dark Challenge by the only medium of Trust in God.

What a Mighty God we Serve, Angels bow before Him, Heaven and Earth Adore Him, what a Mighty God we Serve. I hope that this Message has helped God's People for this New Year and beyond; always I remain your friend, brother and Fellow Servant in The Ministry of God; continue always to offer a word of Prayer for me and my Family and also this Ministry, God Bless. Pastor Lerone Dinnall.

TRUST IN GOD...

God's Favor

Message # 68

Date Started March 7, 2017
Date Finalized March 13, 2017.

I Greet my Lord and Saviour in no other Name but The Name of Jesus Christ; Blessed and Privileged to be writing another Wonderful Message for God's People, to let us know how Blessed we are in The Eyes of God, as long as we do His Will.

According to the Webster's Dictionary, Favor is something done or granted out of goodwill, rather than from justice or for payment; a kind act. Hear is one word we should keep an eye on; that word is called: WHY? Why God's Favor is upon The Righteous Seed? It is because of an Act of Obedience. Man explanation of the word Favor, gives us a mere glimpse of what The Favor of God really means; because while it is that most men will not grant a release of their goodness towards someone else, unless they have proven and are sure that, that individual will be and is of benefit to their lives; in The Eyes of God Granting Favors means a lot more than strings attached. We are living in a World that seeks to Train its occupants that the only way to receive of the best gifts or blessings, is to seek to reach the highest level of Education, or to secure the best paid job, which will result in that person being able to accumulate as much money to buy for themselves happiness. Now those of us who are born in God would have identified that all the material things and the accolades, the best paid job and all the money there is to buy anything we would desire, does not necessarily bring forth the words that spells God's Favor. I will remind my Readers of a Scripture that Says:

"THE BLESSINGS OF THE LORD, IT MAKETH RICH, AND HE ADDETH NO SORROW WITH IT". Proverbs 10:22.

Here is a thought: "CAN THAT WHICH WE POSSESS OR CONSIDER TO BE A BLESSING BE GOD'S FAVOR, IF IT TAKES US OUT OF THE WILL OF GOD"?

There are many Saints that are currently living in God's Favor and don't even realize that we are living in that which add no sorrows; because we are so fueled by the influences of the World, we miss what God has Granted us every Morning, because the Red eye Monster has taken over our Attitude to make us believe that we are still desirous of more than that which God has Allowed for us to have in a Day. The World Teaches by Television, Radio, Internet, our Neighbor next door, Telephone etc. and the Message is clear; having more and more is the best; and even if we already have one item that is working and is in perfect condition; the World Teaches that nothing is wrong to go out of our way to get another item, although we can only use one item at a time. And this event causes us to miss the True Favor of God upon our lives, which God has freely Given unto His People.

It is needless to say that every person has an evidence of God's Favor upon their lives; have you ever notice that wherever we go, there is at least one person in each corner of life, that can bring forth an expression to us that there is A God, and He's Continuing to Do Mighty things all over the World, despite of the devices of the World. God is still Granting Favors, but is our eyes open to discover The Favors that are being Granted daily, and this I speak to a Level. The Effectiveness of God's Favors can be seen and heard when there is a Mumbling and a Murmuring, a Shock of unbelief to the Adversary that says: How has this happen; Why has this Happen; there is no explanation for what happen, for it to happen; why did he or she receive of that blessing; he or she is not qualified to receive such a blessing; there is more persons more qualified than him or her to receive of that opportunity; why; why ; why they asked? The answer is simple: GOD FAVORS ME.

I've gotten to realize and to understand that this life that we are living in is very strange; in the event that it is only design to carry its occupants in a complete circle for a complete lifetime; and each person has to be very careful of how we treat this walk of life; this life is every Child of God Testing Ground, to prove to God that we are worthy to surpass the elements of this life to move to The Home of Eternal Rest. There is a reason and a purpose why God is God, and why it is that only God Alone can be Judge, because God Judges with Equal Rights "EQUITY", which means, everyone will receive of what that person have worked for. Man's rule and favors will always seek to promote the desires of man and will always seek to promote those who are directly in their circle; therefore if someone is more capable and qualified to perform a job with great effectiveness, if that person is not found to be in the circle of the person who is doing the hiring, then automatically, that person will not be getting that job; Not so with God.

To receive another level of Understanding God's Favor; The Lord Revealed that His Favors is DIVINELY FIXED; which means that those who are to receive of, in order to walk in God's Favor, must be those who are PREDESTINATED for such an Anointing. This means that this person, the very moment that The Lord Anoint this person for the Decreed Favors; this blessing is not one that if you take a shower or swim in the sea, can be washed off; instead, this Divine Anointing remains upon the life of this individual for their entire lifetime, and will and must continue for the lifetime of the future Generations to come; being now PERMANENTLY FIXED. What this means is that no matter what this person mistakes in life will be, The Favors of which God has Bestowed upon that person will definitely remain upon that person's life, and nothing can change it until Time has come to an end; it must be noted however that The Favors can be delayed to manifest within the life of this person based on the fact that this person have not yet start to walk in the Responsibilities of this Anointing. And if it is that the Parents of this Anointing Favors of God choose not to uphold or to walk in this Anointing Favors, then the promise of this Anointing Favors is now upon the Children of these parents to now accept the walk of which their Parents was not able, or did not choose to accept to walk in. And such was the destiny of The Children of Israel when they decided not to enter The Promised Land when The Lord Commanded them to go forth and to Inherit; The Blessing remained because it came out of The Mouth of God already as a Promise to Abraham, but that Generation of Parents was not Allowed by God to enter because of a spirit of Disobedience; The Children however of those same Parents was Allowed to enter being the next Generation that choose to Obey God's Command.

Bishop Austin Whitfield would often say:

"WHEN GOD PUT HIS HANDS ON YOU, NO ONE CAN REMOVE IT, BECAUSE GOD'S HAND IS HEAVY".

Have you ever wonder why it is that there is Mountains and there is Valleys, and no matter what takes place upon the Mountain or in the Valley, that event is never strong enough nor can be strong enough to change the status of the Mountain or the Valley, unless it is an Act from God. If we set a Mountain on fire and all the trees be Burned, and the houses on the Mountain are destroyed, after all have been destroyed or damaged, there is still the Mountain that will remain, and over a period of time, that Mountain will again bring forth trees, and houses will again be built, until Time has come to an end; but before Time has ended, that Mountain and Valley would have gone through all Generation and still remain the same status. Therefore being Children of God we can't afford to lose our focused of God, to watch those who are not living right from those who are living right, because that person who our eyes may be fixed on is already Fixed in God, despite of the mistakes that is taking place in their life currently. God Can and will Allow for the Garden to spring again. It is even seen in The Church, those who are Appointed to be Ministers and Missionaries, Evangelist, Pastors, Deacons and Bishops; these Offices are Fixed in God; even if that person have not yet learned what it is to walk in that Office, it's a

Title that remains upon their lives until they come to the understanding of the responsibility to walk in that Position.

Therefore don't become a person who Judge, but rather be fearful, because the day will come that you also will be Appointed for Ministry, and trust me, you're not going to get everything right the first or the second or the third time, because Christianity and Ministry for God is set for a Lifetime and not a week or a Month or a year or years, but instead for a complete lifetime; therefore those of us who are walking in God, must understand that we have a lifetime to get the Christian walk right. And lifetime does not mean that we have time to waste, but instead to drop off daily that we may become The Perfect man in Christ Jesus. We are all aware of the Great Favors that overtook Father Abraham, which was only based on his Obedience; now here is a story of one of Abraham descendants, Namely Joseph; which have received of God's Greatest Favor. One Aspect of Joseph life for receiving God's Favor is because he was of The Inheritance to receive of that Favor; another reason why Joseph was Destined for God's Favor is because he was and remained Disciplined even if death came his way, he was not going to deny The God that he was Serving and The God that his father and his forefather had Served; comes what may, he was going to remain True to his God. This is something we should take note of, if it is that we are desirous of receiving God's Favor; we have got to remain True to God, comes what may, even if our belief leads to our death.

The Lord Said in St. Matthew 10:28. "AND FEAR NOT THEM WHICH KILL THE BODY, BUT ARE NOT ABLE TO KILL THE SOUL: BUT RATHER FEAR HIM WHICH IS ABLE TO DESTROY BOTH SOUL AND BODY IN HELL".

For the story of Joseph, at the end of his trials, Joseph was called to interpret the dream of the king without knowing that his interpretation was going to bring forth the Manifestation of God's Favor. Genesis 41:37-45. There are many times that God Calls us to walk the Test, and we have constantly shy away from walking that Test, not knowing that within the Secrets of all Test that a Child of God face, rest and is waiting for the Birth of The Divine, Destined Favor of God for that Child of God life.

There is a saying that goes like this: "THE DARKEST PART OF THE NIGHT IS WHEN THE DAY IS ABOUT TO BREAK".

I know there are times we look to The Heavens, and it would seem as if we are asking God if He Knows what He is Doing concerning our lives; or if God Sees what is happening to us on the journey of Test that we walk. And this is the time that we must try to remain Focused, and Trust God; because while it is that we are only viewing what is directly in front of us; God Sees our beginning and our ending all in one View, and also knows the Destiny of our Generation to come; therefore worrying about The Test and the Dangers of The Test, should not cause us to lose focused, because God is Faithful. God was Faithful to Abraham, Isaac, Israel, Moses, Joshua, David, Samuel, Daniel, Peter, James, John, and also Paul, and these are but just a few; what about those of us who are Serving God in Spirit and in Truth, in which The Living Spirit of God Dwells; is God not also going to be Faithful to us; think about it!

If it is that we have been going through our Test for a long Season, and to our understanding it would seem best that The Test must end now or very soon; we must understand that The Test is not Fixed to facilitate our desire of when it should end in what period of time, but rather to know that every Test that is given by God for His Children, is for us to Learn of the Lessons that are Affiliated with that Test; therefore the journey and the time spent in each Test is directly dependent on The Child of God that is walking the road of that Test. Here is a Truth, many of God's Children are DUNCE / IGNORANT; and the only way to finish The Test Given is for us to Learn, and for many of us, Learning takes a very long time; and I don't mean that we are Ignorant in this World's knowledge, but rather in The Word of God; because there is many of us that thinks and believe that the Knowledge of this World is of Great merits to God; rather The Lord Said that the wisdom of this World is foolish to The Wisdom of God. Having Education is very good, and is of great benefit; but Education of this World cannot measure or even compare to Spiritual Revelations. Here is a Fact; no one will receive of God's Favor if that person is not fully equipped with The Understanding, Knowledge, and Wisdom of God, which Represents The God Head; to Know exactly how to KEEP that Divine Favor that God Has Given, and this is speaking about Favors that are Fixed, and not necessarily speaking about the daily provisional Favors we experience each day. And to receive of The God Head, it takes for each Child of God to first pass The Test that God has Set for that Servant to pass. Learn this, no one can bypass The Test; as it is that no one can bypass one level of Spirituality to move to another level of Spirituality, unless they go through the Process; as it is also Revealed that no one can Inherit Heaven unless that person have mastered the True Direction of Free Will; which is to know that God is always Right, and Man's way is always wrong, even if it looks like it is right, as long as it does not correspond with what The Word of God Says, that simple demonstration makes it 100% wrong. I know that the World we are living in Teaches us that we can bypass different levels of process, based on the money or influential Background that we have, to pay our way through, but that cannot stand with God. In God's Eyes, No completion of The Test that is Given means that there is no Release of God's Favor; and believe me, reading about God's Favor is more than worth any Test that a Child of God will face.

Reading about The Favors of God is very desirous, but actually being in the position to acquire those Favor, a Child of God has got to be ready to walk and also to fulfill the requirement of every Test that God Will Give for that individual to receive of The Great Favors of God. No Test, No Favors, No Clean Sacrifice, means no Acceptance of the worship we have given to God; which result in no Release of God's Favor for our lives. For those who will receive of God Favors, this Gracious Anointing is one that is embedded in our DNA or Inheritance, because God has already placed a Stamp of Worthy, and this is not because we are Worthy, but rather because our Forefathers have committed some duty of Obedience before God, that cause God to Remember the act of Obedience throughout all Generations. For those of us who will be born to inherit God's Favor; are those who will Touch God through great offences, just like the woman with the issue of blood; she wasn't even supposed to be in the audience of other people with her condition, but that did not stop her from pressing her way through the crowd in order to receive just a Touch, which brought forth a Complete Deliverance / or God's Favor upon her life. So is it with those who are to be born into God's Favor; again it calls for complete Obedience towards that which God would Require of us to Do; and a great level of Discipline for us to press through every obstacles that may prevent us from receiving the achievement of God's Requirement through our Obedience.

It is a joy to know that through my personal Obedience of God's Word for my life, this would have automatically paved the way for all my Children, and for their Children's, Children to enjoy the benefit of a walk with God, that is fulfilled with a lifetime of The Promises of God's Continual Favor upon their lives, if they also choose to walk in the pathway of God's Obedience. This Promise is a Guarantee Assurance from God, that even when my eyes are close, because my work on Earth would have ended; I rest Confidently knowing that God's Favor is upon my Generation to come. The Banks of this World seeks to bring forth an assurance to their Clients that Customer's investments is always safe and will receive various increase as time pass. But who and what can compare to The Guaranteed Favors that God will Fulfill upon our Generation when our eyes are now closed, and there is no more work we can fulfill under the sun? No one, No Organization, No Bank, No Family members, No Husband, No Wife; but only God Alone.

The Word of God Says in Psalms 37:25. "I HAVE BEEN YOUNG, AND NOW AM OLD; YET HAVE I NOT SEEN THE RIGHTEOUS FORSAKEN, NOR HIS SEED BEGGING BREAD".

There is one thing I've gotten to understand about Christianity, and that is, Christianity is bigger than any one individual; Christianity and God's Favors speaks at all times towards the continuation of The Righteous Seed, which is preserve forever, until God has Recognized that He has through His Investment of His Righteous Seed Acquired The Level of Perfection, that our Forefathers was not able to achieved because of the Seed of Envy. Therefore it must be realized by those of us who are reading this Message, that in order for us to have the Guaranteed Assurance, that no Bank can give, is to know for a Fact that not only will our lives be filled with The Favors of God based on our Obedience, but also that our Righteous action for God will result in our Generation, which we will never be able to see, would have also acquired The Great Benefits of having The Stamp of God's Approval, for God's Favor upon their Lives.

Let me end this Message with a Great Advice for all those who are interested to obtain of God's Favor, not only for this present life, but for the life that our Children will live.

The Bible Said in The Book of Proverbs 13:22. "A GOOD MAN LEAVETH AN INHERITANCE TO HIS CHILDREN'S CHILDREN: AND THE WEALTH OF THE SINNER IS LAID UP FOR THE JUST".

The Lord Revealed that the best inheritance a man could ever sow for his Children's, Children; is for that man to walk the road of Obedience towards The Will of God, and by doing this, it will ensure for that man Children's, Children to come, be able to achieve much greater benefits than that which even a Bank can give; because the Bank will change and may even Crash, but God can never Crash; times may and will change, but God always remain the Same.

The Bible mentioned in The Book of St. Matthew 6:19-21. Says: "LAY NOT UP FOR YOURSELVES TREASURES UPON EARTH, WHERE MOTH AND RUST DOTH CORRUPT, AND WHERE THIEVES BREAK THROUGH AND STEAL: BUT LAY UP FOR YOURSELVES TREASURES IN HEAVEN, WHERE NEITHER MOTH NOR RUST DOTH CORRUPT, AND WHERE THIEVES DO NOT BREAK THROUGH NOR STEAL: FOR WHERE YOUR TREASURE IS, THERE WILL YOUR HEART BE ALSO".

Think very closely on what these words are saying. Lord, I remain a Humble Servant in Your Hands, for You to continue to Use me in the way it seems fit in Your Will. I Give All Praise, Honor and Glory, to The King of kings and The Lord of all lords, Jesus Christ, The Saviour of all Mankind. From The Servant of God Pastor Lerone Dinnall.

GOD'S FAVOR.

CONCLUSION

THE GOD OF THE Universe has Given unto His People clear examples within The Words of God, and it is also Revealed through this Book that God is still Mindful of His Creation, with Desiring to always choose the pathway of Mercy and Forgiveness, to allow the gathering of those People who will choose to change, to now have the pardon Granted to become Children of The Kingdom of God.

God's Desire is always Good towards His People, therefore we must be born in The Understanding to know that a life from God will only spell the words Destruction. It is evidently seen in The Book of Judges; whenever The Children of Israel did what God Commanded them to Do, they prospered in everything that their hands touched, but when The Children of Israel forsook The Commandments of God, and walked away from The Training that was to be Maintained by their Teachers, it was then observed that God Brought evil upon all those who Desired not to follow or to Maintain The Disciplines of The Almighty God.

It is my Prayer that every Soul that comes in contact with the Reading and Revelations of this Book, will become one more Person that will be Born for The Glory and The Manifestation of God's Kingdom, not only for yourself, but also for your Generation.

All Glory be given to The King of kings and The Lord of lords, The God of Abraham, The God of Isaac, The God of Israel; unto The only God that Declares that He is Alpha and Omega, The First and The Last; The God that Liveth and Died, and now is Alive forever more, Jesus Christ The Lamb of God.

From The Ministry Of The Church Of Jesus Christ Fellowship Savannah Cross Ltd. Jamaica West Indies. GOD BLESS.